Two week loan

Please return on or before the last
date stamped below.
Charges are made for late return.

8 FEB 1999 CANCELLED	07 MAY 2002	
23 MAR 1999 CANCELLED		
15 APR 1999		
CANCELLED		
3 NOV 1999 CANCELLED		
0 6 DEC 1999		
15 SEP 2000		
15 SEP 2000 CANCELLED	WITHDRAWN	
26 NOV 2001 CANCELLED		

LF 114/0796

Sex and the Workplace

*The Impact
of Sexual Behavior and Harassment
on Women, Men, and Organizations*

Barbara A. Gutek

Sex and the Workplace

 Jossey-Bass Publishers

San Francisco • London • 1985

SEX AND THE WORKPLACE
The Impact of Sexual Behavior and Harassment
on Women, Men, and Organizations
by Barbara A. Gutek

Copyright © 1985 by: Jossey-Bass Inc., Publishers
433 California Street
San Francisco, California 94104
&
Jossey-Bass Limited
28 Banner Street
London EC1Y 8QE

Library of Congress Cataloging-in-Publication Data

Gutek, Barbara A.
  Sex and the workplace.

  (Jossey-Bass management series) (Jossey-Bass social
and behavioral science series)
  Bibliography: p. 203.
  Includes index.
  1. Sexual harassment of women.   2. Sex discrimination
in employment.   3. Organizational behavior.   I. Title.
II. Title: Sex and the work place.   III. Series.
IV. Series: Jossey-Bass social and behavioral science series.
HD6060.3.G88   1985   305.4'3   85-45054
ISBN 0-87589-656-1

Manufactured in the United States of America

JACKET DESIGN BY WILLI BAUM

FIRST EDITION
Code 8531

A joint publication in
The Jossey-Bass
Social and Behavioral Science Series
and
The Jossey-Bass Management Series

Preface

Sex and the workplace. The words connote a sexy image that sounds like fun. The image also sounds frivolous, not worthy of the attention of serious professionals. Because of this seeming frivolity, sex at work has not been closely examined, and we know little about it beyond our own experiences and a few widely publicized, often scandalous events.

Because of various social forces, we are now learning about sex at work and have discovered that it is not a rare phenomenon. Sex is manifest in various ways at work, from sexual relationships between workers to flirtatious conversations, pictures and posters, jokes, and styles of dress. Over 80 percent of workers report some kind of "social-sexual" experience on their jobs. Even more important, such experiences can be—and are—a problem for workers and for organizations; in fact, I have found sex at work a problem for up to half of all workers—not surprisingly, for many more women than men. The amount and kind of social-sexual behavior frequently go beyond any natural attraction between two people. It is a mistake to assume that sex at work is simply a product of biological attraction between men and women and that none of it has work-related consequences.

This book reports my investigation of the effects of sex at work on individuals and organizations. I show that sex is a "normal" part of people's behavior at work in that it is a common occurrence; I also show that it has considerable impact. Specifically, sex at work has two kinds of effects, and the goals of this book are to elucidate both of them. One goal is to explore how and why sex becomes a tangible problem for individuals and organizations. The other goal is to demonstrate its subtle effects, ones that are not defined as problems but that have pervasive influences on individuals and organizations and that provide the settings in which problems develop.

These effects are important for several reasons. First, they enrich our understanding of organizational behavior and the dynamics of social interaction at work. Second, they are useful input for organizational change aimed at eliminating problematic sex from the work environment. My experience with sexual harassment court cases suggests that an understanding of sex at work, of the ways organizations unwittingly encourage problematic behavior, and of methods of managing potential problems probably could prevent many financially and psychologically costly lawsuits.

To help understand sex at work, I frame the issue within the perspective of sex role spillover. That concept, first used by Nieva and Gutek (1981), emphasizes the sex roles all of us are expected to adopt and the way these sex roles "spill over" and interfere with work roles. In Chapter One, I explain why this happens and how it relates to sex at work. In the rest of the book, I use the concept of sex role spillover to organize material and to show how this spillover quietly shapes the work experiences of both sexes and occasionally creates problems for workers and organizations.

Sex and the Workplace represents the culmination of a comprehensive program of research on sex at work and the interactions of women and men at work. The book is based on findings from several studies, primarily from a large random-sample survey of 1,257 working men and women in Los Angeles County. An advantage of this random-sample method is that it yields generalizable information on sexual behavior, including sexual harassment, which workers have such problems, how they react, and, most important, the kind of organizational conditions that foster such problems.

In the process of researching *Sex and the Workplace,* I have given talks to various professional and business organizations, served as an expert witness in court cases, and consulted with companies about sex at work. I have also had many lively discussions with academic and business colleagues about the implications of my research. This book thus presents not only the findings of several research studies but also interpretation of those findings and implications for working women and men as well as for organizations.

Several audiences should find this material of particular interest: (1) Psychologists and other social and management scientists who want to extend what we know about workers' behavior will be especially interested in the subtle but pervasive effects of sex at work. (2) Organizational specialists and consultants, including organizational development professionals, may have both academic and practical concerns about sex at work and its implications for individuals and organizations. (3) Personnel administrators and other human resources professionals and managers who want to promote healthy work environments, and who often have to deal with problems associated with sex at work, will find the implications for management and recommendations especially relevant. (4) Counseling psychologists and therapists on staffs of organizations, on college campuses, and in private practice often have clients who are sexually harassed or uncomfortable with sexuality at their workplace or campus; they will find both the theoretical and practical aspects useful. And (5) feminist writers and members of the legal profession who have been pushing for awareness of sexual harassment, relief for victims, and remedies for the problem will find the theoretical perspective and recommendations for action pertinent to their concerns.

Overview of the Contents

The first chapter provides a brief historical overview. It then focuses on the way feminists, lawyers, companies, and others have addressed the issue of sex at work, explanations for its existence, the theoretical perspective I developed, and a brief description of the research methods.

Because work provides the context for sexuality in this study, Chapter Two explores the general issue of men's work and women's work. The extent of sex segregation of work and pay differentials of men and women have been widely researched and discussed. This chapter emphasizes how these differences—especially sex segregation—affect the psychological experiences of working women and men. The simple fact that most men have never had a female supervisor, for example, colors their reactions to women as workers. Likewise, the fact that many women have never had a male subordinate affects their reactions to men at work.

Exploring the extent and frequency of social-sexual behavior at work, the third chapter emphasizes sexual harassment, focusing on how large and important this problem is and who the most likely victims are.

The next chapter follows directly from the third by examining the characteristics of harassers and studying the reactions of victims of harassment. One of Chapter Four's conclusions is that it is not possible to identify specific characteristics of male harassers. Men who harass women look much like other working men. Women who have been harassed are concerned that they will be blamed for the incident, but they are also concerned that the harasser's career might be damaged. These two concerns, along with their strong belief that the organization will not correct the situation, generally keep women from making any formal complaints. The findings in the third and fourth chapters are consistent with the sex role spillover perspective.

Representing another angle on the issue of sex and the workplace, Chapter Five is an analysis of the verbatim comments of men and women who report sexual overtures from the other sex. Their comments reflect their own feelings on the subject; some show slight embarrassment and others exhibit humor or earthiness. Some of the comments were expected (for example, a fear that some workers are willing to trade sexual favors for privileges and rewards at work), but others were unexpected. For example, I found that some workers can engage in rather extreme sexual behavior if they manage to convince the target person that it is "only a joke."

The sixth chapter moves away from behavior to people's attitudes. Most workers tend to think that people who are targets of sexual overtures could avoid them if they wanted to, that workers dress to be attractive to the other sex, and that some even dress to be seductive. One of the study's more interesting findings reveals a giant gender gap in attitudes. Men consistently say they are flattered by sexual overtures from women. Women consistently say they are insulted by sexual propositions from men.

Chapter Seven more systematically examines the role of the workplace in people's experiences. Not surprisingly, those work environments that are especially characterized by sex role spillover, that is, where the work role is deemphasized and the sex role is exaggerated, tend to have more social-sexual behavior. People respond to the expectations generated within their work environments. Furthermore, highly sexualized environments affect women's job satisfaction; the more sexualized the environment, the lower their job satisfaction.

The earlier chapters generally support the spillover perspective, while Chapter Eight examines a specific hypothesis about sex ratios and sex role spillover. I argue that sex segregation of work leads to sex role spillover and to sexuality in the workplace. The findings show that where men and women work together in equal numbers in the same jobs, there are virtually no social-sexual problems.

Each of these chapters contains important differences between the sexes in attitudes, behavior, definitions, reactions, and explanations. These findings can be summarized in the following short statement: In general, women are hurt by sex in the workplace but men are not. The findings further suggest what some people might consider an outrageous statement: Contrary to popular belief, women do not use sex at work nearly as frequently as men do. Men talk about sex more and use it to express a variety of feelings—friendship, caring, power, dominance, and hostility—toward women and to advertise their heterosexuality to other men. This "outrageous" statement and other findings, the subtle effects of sex at work, are summarized under various themes in the last chapter: the seriousness of harassment as a social problem, the pervasiveness of sexuality in our society, the invisibility of social structure, our concept of male and female sex roles, and the trivializing effects of sex. Many implications for managing the problem of sex are also included in Chapter Nine, which concludes with some specific suggestions for eliminating sexual harassment at work.

In sum, *Sex and the Workplace* uses six years of methodologically solid research to describe and explain an area of organizational behavior about which we know little: sex at work. Two effects of sex at work provide the focus for the book: (1) sex as a problem for workers, managers, human resources specialists, lawyers, feminists, counselors, consultants, and perhaps others and (2) sex as a subtle, pervasive influence that quietly shapes people's experiences at work, their reactions to others, and their views of themselves.

Sex as a problem is insistent and clamors for attention. It has received a lion's share of publicity but has often been handled clumsily and poorly. Sex as a subtle influence is almost invisible. So far, it has not been acknowledged, and its effects are largely unknown.

Acknowledgments

Many people contributed to this effort. First, the Center for Work and Mental Health of the National Institute of Mental Health, under the direction of Eliot Liebow, deserves thanks for supporting the research reported here (funded under grant USPHS-MH-32606-01). Special thanks go to Maury Lieberman for his comments, criticism, encouragement, and help on this project. The research reported here relies heavily on the skills and knowledge I acquired at the Institute for Social Research at the University of Michigan, especially through working with Daniel Katz and Robert Kahn. This project and I have also benefited from my collaboration with Veronica Nieva on several projects.

I began this project at the University of California at Los Angeles, continued it at the Claremont Graduate School, and finally finished it on sabbatical in West Germany. Several people at the University of California at Los Angeles contributed substantially to this project, especially in the early stages. I especially thank Jackie Goodchilds, who encouraged me to pursue this research, and Charles Nakamura, whose efforts greatly contributed to getting the project off the ground. At the University of California at Los Angeles, Inger Jensen, Bruce Morasch, and Paul Phillips each added substantially to the total project. At the Claremont Graduate School, numerous people made contributions: Aaron Cohen, Pam Cooper, Vera Dunwoody-Miller, Alison Konrad, Linda Mitchell, Lynn Savitzky, and Roberta Valdez. I also thank the Claremont Graduate School, the Alexander von Humboldt Foundation of West Germany, and the Institute for Work Physiology (Institut für Arbeitsphysiologie) at the University of Dortmund in West Germany for providing the resources to allow me to finish the book free from other obligations. Preparation of the manuscript was ably handled by Zulma Duran at the University of California at Los Angeles, Jane Grey at Claremont Graduate School, and my personal computer at home.

Finally, I thank Rachel and Christopher for not harassing me while I was working on this project and Geza Bottlik for his support (who, even though he never offered to type my manuscript, did fix my computer).

Claremont, California   Barbara A. Gutek
August 1985

Contents

The Author

Barbara A. Gutek is associate professor of psychology, business administration, and executive management at the Claremont Graduate School. She received her A.B. degree from the University of Michigan (1971) in psychology and sociology and her Ph.D. degree from the University of Michigan in psychology (1975), specializing in organizational psychology.

Gutek's main research activities, focusing on work, include the study of job satisfaction, survey research methods in the study of organizational behavior, the social impacts of computerization of work, bureaucracy, and women and work. Gutek's books and monographs are *Bureaucratic Encounters* (1975, with Daniel Katz, Robert Kahn, and Eugenia Barton), *Enhancing Women's Career Development* (1979), *Women and Work* (1981, with Veronica Nieva), and *Sex Role Stereotyping and Affirmative Action Policy* (1982). She is coeditor with Laurie Larwood and Ann Stromberg of *Women and Work: An Annual Review;* the first volume will appear in 1985.

Sex and the Workplace

*The Impact
of Sexual Behavior and Harassment
on Women, Men, and Organizations*

ONE

Sex and the Workplace: The Issues

Mary was hired as a secretary at a large insurance company. To her dismay, she found that her boss asked her to work late with him on several projects. He spent much of this time telling her about his personal problems, including his unsatisfactory relationship with his wife. He usually apologized for keeping her at work so late and offered to take her to dinner. Mary refused each time but still felt uncomfortable. After three weeks, although she did not have another job offer, she quit.

Jane and Tom, junior engineers at a large aerospace company, were assigned to the same project and found that they enjoyed working together. They were frequently the last two project members to leave, discussing fine points of their work at the end of the day. No one in the company was surprised when they announced their engagement eight months later.

When Jennie applied for the job as an operator of a forklift truck, the personnel manager said the job was no place for a "lady" because workers used crude language and pinups were posted throughout the plant. Jennie said she didn't mind. After she started the job, she felt uncomfortable and unwanted. Her male colleagues never used crude language with her; they ignored her completely. The pinups bothered her more than she thought. After a month, resentful toward her male peers and disappointed in herself, Jennie quit the job.

1

Mike, a professor at a university, is recently divorced. Attracted to a student in his class, although she was his daughter's age, he called on her frequently and often spoke to her at the end of class. When the semester was over, he asked her to come over for dinner. Three weeks later, she moved in with him.

Anita works in a warehouse. She is not married and has a two-year-old daughter. The men in the warehouse frequently make crude comments to Anita and often talk about her in her presence using explicit sexual language. Anita feels that these comments are obnoxious but part of the job.

Sex and work are believed to be about as compatible as oil and water. Still, occasionally something sexual happens at work, and many people can recount incidents like the vignettes just presented. The expression of sexuality at work might be in the form of sexual attraction between two people, as in the case of Jane and Tom, or it might involve one-sided attraction. That attraction might be pursued outside of the workplace, or the interested party could use work to create opportunities to further his or her interests, as Mary's boss did. In the most extreme case, an initiator with some power over the other person could require that person to engage in sexual relations to keep a job or be promoted.

Sexuality at work can take other forms, such as the sexual jokes and comments, whistles, innuendos, staring, and touching experienced by Anita. Sexuality can be emphasized by tight or revealing clothing, which is sometimes the job's required uniform (for example, for a cocktail waitress) or the employee's own selection. Sexuality is also manifested through pinups or posters around the workplace or voluntary disclosure of intimate information. All of these have been called social-sexual behaviors; they are not related to work and have both a social aspect and a sexual aspect (see Gutek and others, 1980; Gutek and Nakamura, 1982). This book is based on an ongoing program of research that started in 1978 focusing on male-female relations in the workplace. It is a unique empirical study of an area about which we know little.

Knowing about sex at work is important because it affects people and organizations directly and indirectly. It affects people's job satisfaction and career advancement, as well as an organization's image and its productivity. In particular, sex at work is a problem for individuals who receive unwelcome sexual advances or who feel required to make sexual overtures and for managers and personnel administrators who must sort out messy situations and try to treat everyone fairly without disrupting work. Knowing about sex at work is also important for therapists, lawyers, researchers, and academicians.

The study of sex at work uses the concepts of sex roles and gender. Because these concepts are sometimes quite vague, it is important to define them. Recently researchers and theoreticians have distinguished between sex and gender. Lipman-Blumen (1984), for example, uses sex to refer to biologically based differences such as menstruation, lactation, or ejaculation, and gender to refer to societally based differences such as who has primary care of the children. That distinction is not always followed in this book because the use of the word *sex* to refer to men and women (the two sexes) and a broad class of behavior (sex at the workplace) can be confusing. In an effort to be clear, I use the word *sex* and sometimes *sexuality* to describe the subject of this book and *sex* or *gender* to refer to men and women and the differences between them, whether societally or biologically based. Thus, the traditional term *sex role* and the newer term *gender role* are both used to refer to behavior expected of men or women in our society.

Impact of the Increase in Working Women

The possibility for more sexual activity at work follows from the growth of women's involvement in the labor force. Over 50 percent of adult women are currently in the labor force, up from 32 percent in 1960 (U.S. Department of Labor, 1983). Economists, who generally underestimated the number of women who would enter the job market during the 1970s, now believe that the percentage of women in the labor force will increase throughout the 1980s and 1990s (Flaim and Fullerton, 1978). The more men and women come into contact at work, the greater the potential for expressions of sexuality, especially if women continue to join the labor force in positions of relatively low status and low power.

Unfortunately, that is the case (Macke, 1982). While much of the popular and academic literature focuses on women in high-status, high-prestige jobs, most women are still entering the labor force at low levels. Furthermore, women's salaries relative to men's salaries have not increased appreciably (U.S. Department of Labor, 1980). Although recent reports suggest some improvement (Pennar and Mervosh, 1985), the rate still hovers around 62 percent; that is, for every $1 the average man earns, the average women receives $.62.

The current direction of women's employment—more women entering traditional women's work than nontraditional work—suggests that more men and women will spend time at work together but in different jobs. Men's jobs will be relatively high status or high paying compared to women's, and most of the other people in a man's type of job, including his supervisor, will be men. In contrast, most working women will work with other women but will have a male supervisor; their work will be relatively low status and poorly paid. In addition, some women will be working in traditionally male jobs, and they will interact often with men who are peers and supervisors, and even with some who are subordinates.

The Invisibility of Sexuality at Work

Although sexuality has probably always been present at work, it has been practically invisible. Presumably, in the past, people thought such activities were relatively infrequent and, when they did occur, had only minor repercussions both for the individuals involved and for the organization where they worked. The idea of frequent occurrence of sex at work was at odds with rational models of organizational behavior. From Weber's concept of bureaucratic rationality as a model of organization to current individual-level theories of motivation in organizations that stress goal setting and the relationship between work behavior and expected rewards, theories of organization do not provide much room for the expression of sexuality. (See Khandwalla, 1977, or Pfeffer, 1982, for comprehensive discussions of organizational theories.) Sexuality is emotional, not rational. It may be an important aspect of life, but can be viewed as a frivolous concern at work compared to weighty matters of commerce, government, and education. Thus, an organization viewing itself as rational may respond to any expression of sexuality at work by ignoring, overlooking, suppressing, or denying it.

Besides the incompatibility of expressions of sexuality with models of organizational behavior, sex at work has been almost invisible for other reasons. In the male-dominated world of work, the woman is viewed as "sexual." Her presence elicits the expression of sexuality. Removing the sexual woman from the setting restores an asexual environment. For example, in the past, when two employees in an organization married, the wife frequently left the organization voluntarily, at her husband's insistence, or because of the organization's regulations. Thus, the "evidence" of a sexual liaison—that is, the woman—is no longer "at the scene of the crime." Relationships lacking happy endings also are quickly forgotten since one of the parties—almost always the woman—quits the job, is transferred, or is asked to leave.

Although the literature on organizational behavior ignores the existence of sexuality in the workplace, evidence for its occurrence might come from other sources. However, evidence that sexuality occurs at work also is noticeably absent from research on dating, marriage, and rape. Research on dating and courtship does not mention work particularly as an important place to make such contacts. Nor does the workplace figure prominently in the literature on rape. Although there are some rapes at work, the majority of rapes occur elsewhere.

Sexual Harassment

The issue of sexuality in the workplace became visible and was brought to public attention in the form of sexual harassment. The first accounts of sexual harassment were journalistic reports and case studies (Safran, 1976; Lindsey, 1977; Pogrebin, 1977). The first large-scale, systematic analysis of the problem was Farley's (1978) *Sexual Shakedown: The Sexual Harassment of Women on the Job,* a book that defined the concept and provided numerous examples of harassment of women in a variety of jobs and situations.

Farley's book was followed closely by MacKinnon's (1979) *Sexual Harassment of Working Women*; MacKinnon, an attorney, was interested not only in publicizing the existence of sexual harassment but also in providing a basis for legal action to combat sexual harassment. In a strong and convincing argument, MacKinnon contended that sexual harassment was primarily a problem for women, that it rarely happened to men, and, therefore, that it should be considered a form of sex discrimination. Viewing sexual harassment as a form of sex discrimination would give victims of sexual harassment the same legal protection available to victims of sex discrimination. In the past few years, the Equal Employment Opportunity Commission (EEOC), the agency of the federal government concerned with ensuring equality of opportunity, has established guidelines consistent with MacKinnon's position.

The attention paid to the phenomenon of sexual harassment has raised a number of issues. One concerns the frequency of sexual harassment cases. Of course, it was possible to dredge up horror stories about women's experiences of sexual harassment, but they were isolated instances, said some observers. Others thought that sexual harassment was much more common, and they worried about the courts being overrun with sexual harassment cases. Defining sexual harassment and encouraging victims to come forward was tantamount to opening the floodgates.

One thorny issue is the definition of sexual harassment. Should sexual harassment be limited to forced sexual relations? Should it be limited to situations of unequal power, that is, supervisor-subordinate relationships? Can a worker harass a coworker or only a subordinate? How about touching, cornering, leering, staring, obscene gestures, comments, jokes? Do these constitute sexual harassment? Can a person be harassed without one specific harasser? That is, can the workplace be so uncomfortable and degrading that a person can be harassed even though no one makes comments or gestures directed at that person?

One definition commonly used, "unwanted sexual overtures," has the virtue of parsimony but necessarily concerns intentions and motivation, not just overt behavior. Defining sexual harassment as unwanted sexual overtures has the same problem inherent in defining rape as unwanted sexual relations. In practice, the woman has to prove that the sexual relations or the sexual overtures were unwanted (Burt, 1980).

The EEOC's broad definition of sexual harassment goes beyond interpersonal behavior to include the workplace climate. The commission stated that an intimidating environment constitutes sexual harassment; furthermore, supervisors are responsible when their subordinates are sexually harassed, even when they do not know about the specific instance or instances of harassment. (See Equal Employment Opportunity Commission, 1980; Pearman and Lebrato, 1984.)

In focusing on the work environment, the EEOC recognized that sexual harassment is not just an event between two people. The work environment where sexual harassment occurs has a hierarchy, norms, rules, and constraints that profoundly affect the way people behave in that setting. In particular, the formal rules and informal norms of managers affect everyone in the work group: the managers, their subordinates, their subordinates' subordinates. Thus, top management has the power to influence employees' work habits, style of dress, recreational interests, and social behavior. When top management tolerates or condones sexual harassment of employees, that standard reverberates throughout the organization.

Defining *sexual harassment* means setting boundaries on the term, differentiating sexual harassment from expressions of sexual interest. Not all expressions of sexuality in the workplace could possibly be called sexual harassment. Men and women do meet dating partners and future spouses at work. Some people may enjoy sexual jokes and flirting that can be ego enhancing and enrich their fantasy life. Other people may willingly exchange sexual favors or the promise of sexual favors for privileges at work or the promise of privileges at work (Quinn, 1977). Should some or all of these expressions of sexuality be encouraged by organizations, merely tolerated, discouraged, or forbidden by company regulations? Some of these enjoyable experiences may make people better workers, or they may simply distract people from their assigned tasks. Some of these forms of sexuality may enliven the workday, or they may add stress to an already stressful job.

In addition, even expressions of sexual interest that may be welcomed by the individual are not always in the best interests of the organization (Gutek and Nakamura, 1982). For example, some people who command organizational resources may squander them in attempts to attract desirable sexual partners. Others use organizational resources to impress and entertain potential sexual partners.

The law provides relatively little guidance for organizations in these matters. The EEOC has no guidelines about mutually entered sexual relationships as long as they do not affect people's work. If or how an organization handles dating between employees or marriage between coworkers is not a concern of government agencies unless the policy unfairly discriminates. In the past, employers did not have policies about sexual harassment, but they did have policies about dating and marriage. Teachers could be dismissed if they were dating, and several generations of women were expected to leave their jobs when they put on a wedding ring.

Perspectives on Sexuality at Work

Over the past ten years in the United States, sexuality at work has become the concern of three different groups, each approaching the issue from a different point of view. These three perspectives on the issue include a feminist perspective, a legal perspective, and a management perspective (see the following list, adapted from Gutek, 1982, p. 145). These points of view are neither independent nor mutually exclusive. Some lawyers are feminists, many feminists are managers, and some lawyers are managers.

Sexual Harassment from a Feminist Perspective

- Reflects a power relationship, male over female
- Constitutes economic coercion
- Threatens women's economic livelihood

- Reflects the status of women in society
- Asserts the woman's sex role over her work role
- Parallels rape

Sexual Harassment from a Legal Perspective

- Reflects an unequal power relationship that is exploitative
- Involves both implicit and explicit terms of employment
- Is used as a basis for employment decisions
- Produces consequences from submission to, or refusal of, advances
- Promotes an intimidating, hostile, or offensive work environment

Sexual Harassment from an Organizational Perspective—One View

- Is interpersonal
- Consists of misperception or misunderstanding of a person's intentions
- Is a result of a "love affair gone sour"
- Is personal and therefore not the organization's business
- May be considered normal behavior at work
- Can hurt the reputation of the accused

Sexual Harassment from an Organizational Perspective—Another View

- Is interpersonal
- Is the improper use of power to extort sexual gratification
- Treats women as sex objects
- Is coercive, exploitative, improper
- Asserts the women's sex role over work role
- Is aberrant behavior

The feminist perspective considers social changes necessary to eliminate sexual harassment, while the legal and organizational perspectives seek solutions through changes in the workplace. These changes could include establishing regulations about personal behavior or sanctions for misusing power.

Each perspective is presented in its purest or strongest form; not all feminists, lawyers, or managers would agree with them exactly as they are presented here. This presentation is intended to underscore the divergence in thinking and to gain an appreciation of how difficult it is to deal with the issue in a way that will satisfy all three groups. Understanding the different perspectives is also important because, as Nieva and Gutek (1981, p. 120) pointed out, the way the problem is framed determines the proposed solutions: "The model one adopts to explain women's work situation dictates one's prescriptions for change."

The Feminist Perspective. This wide-ranging perspective sees sexual harassment as a logical consequence of sexism in society. It is both a cause and an effect. Sexual harassment exists because women are considered the inferior sex. Men can exploit women with impunity, in the workplace and outside it. Sexual harassment is also a cause; its occurrence helps to maintain gender stratification. Feminists would view sexual harassment as analogous to rape. Rivers (1978) expressed this viewpoint in her article "Sexual Harassment: The Executive's Alternative to Rape."

One of the ways gender stratification is maintained is by emphasizing sex role expectations. Being a sex object is part of the female sex role. Sexual harassment is a reminder to women of their status as sex objects; even at work, women are sex objects. Feminists would contend that when women behave in a seductive manner at work or are willing to exchange sexual favors for privileges, they do so because they are rewarded more for that behavior than they are for competence at work.

Because sexual harassment is an outgrowth of societal gender stratification, its occurrence in organizations might be viewed as normal or expectable by nonfeminists. At the very least, handling sexual harassment would be viewed by nonfeminists as women's responsibility. If a woman wishes to venture into the world of work, she should expect overtures from men and be able to handle them. This is the general attitude of managers who responded to a survey sent to readers of the *Harvard Business Review:* women should be able to handle whatever comes their way (Collins and Blodgett, 1981). Thus, feminists would contend that sexual harassment is difficult to treat because it is not always viewed as a problem. Accordingly, they are committed to documenting the existence of harassment and exposing it as a form of male domination over women.

Because the feminist perspective sees sexual harassment as an outgrowth of sexism in society, it has relatively little to say about the workplace itself. The workplace is just another sphere of male domination and another arena—like marriage—where men can exert their power over women.

The Legal Perspective. Still in the process of development, the legal perspective on sexual harassment currently parallels the legal approach to sex discrimination. The focus is on the effects of harassment. Sexual harassment occurs when compliance with sexual requests serves as a basis for employment decisions, such as employee selection, performance appraisal, merit increases, promotions, or tenure. Sexual harassment occurs when the offending behavior affects an employee's job performance, mental or physical health, or job satisfaction. Any particular behavior is harassment when it leads to negative consequences for the worker or puts members of that worker's group—in this case, women— at a disadvantage relative to other groups, that is, men.

While the legal perspective recognizes the contribution of societal influences to sexual harassment, it focuses on behavior in the work environment. Thus, complying with the legal requirements necessitates some changes in regulations and actions in the workplace. The employing organization must try to create an environment free of harassment and to respond vigorously to complaints of sexual harassment.

The Management Perspective. The management perspective comes in two variants, one old and the other relatively new. The older variant would not take the existence of sexual harassment very seriously: Sexual interactions are personal matters that occasionally get out of hand. For example, perhaps a woman cannot handle the office "Don Juan" or perhaps he becomes too aggressive with too many female employees. This point of view might also see an allegation of sexual harassment as an outgrowth of a lovers' quarrel or a result of misunderstandings or misperceptions. A woman might be insulted by a remark that was meant to be a compliment. Women's accusations of sexual harassment would arise from their own (1) inability to handle men who are a "little too friendly," (2) sensitivity or modesty about sexuality, or (3) rejection by the man they have accused. This viewpoint is reflected in the saying, "Hell hath no fury like a woman scorned."

Under this point of view, protecting the reputation of the high-status person—almost always a man—from unwarranted accusations that could damage his career may be the organization's prime responsibility. Allegations of harassment are usually handled informally since they are viewed as personal, not organizational, matters. The accuser may be transferred or fired; sometimes the accused may be moved or fired. Since the organization is primarily concerned with retaining the services of the most valuable of the two employees, the high-status person usually stays. Thus, even when the accuser is acknowledged as having a legitimate case, the accuser still may be transferred or asked to leave. For example, a woman who is now an attorney told me that when she was working as a secretary twenty years ago and complained of sexual harassment by her boss, his supervisor told her that she was much more easily replaced than her boss and if she could not handle him, she should look for another job.

The second, newer management point of view takes sexual harassment more seriously. It is viewed as an interpersonal phenomenon, but one that is the organization's business. One person misuses the power associated with his or her organizational position. Sexual harassment is viewed as an expression of personal proclivities in an exploitative way. It is aberrant and unprofessional behavior.

Such an organization might use classes, seminars, and written statements to point out that such behavior is unprofessional and will not be tolerated. The organization can establish an office to handle cases of sexual harassment and to provide counseling to the harasser and the harassed.

Finding a Model for Studying Sex at Work

Underlying the three points of view just described are sets of assumptions about why sexuality exists at work. Examining these sets of assumptions or explanations and the available evidence for each should lead to a useful model or framework for studying sex in the workplace.

After examining the literature on women's work status, Nieva and Gutek (1981) identified four general models or explanations for women's work situation: the individual deficit model, the structural institutional model, the sex role model, and the intergroup model. Each model has different implications for changing women's work status. Concerned more specifically with sexual harassment, Tangri, Burt, and Johnson (1982) examined legal briefs, feminist writings, and popular accounts of sexual harassment. From this literature, they were able to identify three models or explanations for sexuality at work: the natural-biological model, the organizational model, and the sociocultural model. They then examined data collected from the U.S. Merit Systems Protection Board (1981) study of federal employees to evaluate the validity of the three models. What follows is an attempt to integrate these two sets of models—one fairly general and the other more specific—and put together a framework for studying sexuality in the workplace.

The Natural-Biological Model. The natural-biological model assumes that sexual harassment and other forms of sexual expression at work are simply manifestations of natural attraction between two people. It is not sexist or discriminatory and does not have harmful consequences. Most of all, there is no intent to harass. According to Tangri, Burt, and Johnson (1982), one version of this model suggests that because men have a stronger sex drive, they more often initiate sexual overtures, at work as well as in other settings.

This model is compatible with the individual deficit explanation, identified by Nieva and Gutek (1981), which maintains that the sexual harassment women experience is a function of their own deficiency or the deficiency of individual men. Either the woman is incapable of handling an overture or she is overly sensitive. A man may be too assertive or unable to properly control his sex drive. This explanation thus underlies the older management perspective on harassment described earlier.

Tangri, Burt, and Johnson found little evidence to support the natural-biological (or individual deficit) explanation for the existence of sexual harassment. Evidence supporting the model included the findings that most victims of harassment are not married and tend to be young workers.

The Organizational Model. The organizational perspective assumes that sexual harassment is the result of certain opportunity structures within organizations such as hierarchy. People in higher positions can use their authority—that is, legitimate power—and their status to coerce lower-status people into accepting a role of sex object or engaging in sexual interactions. Tangri, Burt, and Johnson (1982) note that the organizational perspective, in its various versions, may or may not take into account the way men and women are distributed throughout the organization's hierarchy.

The organizational model is complemented by Nieva and Gutek's structural institutional model, "which focuses on the impact that work organizations have on the people in them and on the ways in which the people eventually reflect their situations in their behavior" (1981, p. 116). In addition, to the extent that this model takes into account the differential distribution of men and women in organizations, it is also compatible with Nieva and Gutek's intergroup model, focusing on the relationships between males and females as groups. They asserted that "intergroup relations tend to create hierarchical relationships between the groups. In the workplace . . . male characteristics set the norms for 'goodness' from which deviance becomes defined as deficit" (1981, p. 118).

The organizational model appears to underlie some of the viewpoints of both the legal perspective and the newer management perspective described earlier. Tangri, Burt, and Johnson found some support for the organizational model as an explanation for the existence of sexual harassment, but other predictions were not upheld. They concluded that it was useful but only when used in conjunction with other models.

The Sociocultural Model. The third model, the sociocultural one, "argues that sexual harassment reflects the larger society's differential distribution of power and status between the sexes" (Tangri, Burt, and Johnson, 1982, p. 56). Harassment is viewed as a mechanism for maintaining male dominance over women, in work and in society more generally. According to this model, male dominance is maintained by patterns of male-female interaction, as well as by male domination of economic and political matters. Society rewards males for assertive and aggressive sexual behavior and rewards women for being acquiescent, compliant, and passive. This model mirrors the feminist perspective described earlier.

The sociocultural model is compatible with aspects of the sex role explanation and the intergroup explanation described by Nieva and Gutek (1981, p. 117): "The focus of the third [sex role] model is the degree of congruence between a woman's exhibited behaviors or attitudes and those prescribed by general sex role ideals, or those appropriate to specific female roles such as wife, mother, and sex object."

The intergroup model shows that treatment of an individual depends critically on group membership. Thus, the point that a woman may be treated as a sex object, whereas a man in the same job may not, follows from both the sex role and the intergroup models.

Like the organizational model, the sociocultural model fared reasonably well under empirical analysis. However, Tangri, Burt, and Johnson (1982) found that many of the predictions of the sociocultural model were not substantiated by the data of the U.S. Merit Systems Protection Board. People's attitudes, in particular, were not congruent with the sociocultural explanation of sexual harassment.

In conclusion, none of the three models can by itself offer an adequate explanation for sexual harassment; they are also unlikely to be able to explain the broader concept of sexuality. The natural-biological model, which was least successful in explaining sexual harassment, might be more useful in explaining expressions of sexual interest. Thus, a model that combines some of each of their characteristics might explain more. Gutek and Morasch (1982) proposed such a model, emphasizing the effects of sex role expectations in an organizational context. This explanation is called sex role spillover.

The Sex Role Spillover Model. Sex role spillover is a term used by Nieva and Gutek (1981) to denote the carryover into the work-

place of gender-based roles that are usually irrelevant or inappropriate to work. Sex role spillover occurs, for example, when
women are expected to be more nurturant or loyal than men in
the same position. Sex role spillover also occurs when women are
expected to serve as helpers (as in laboratory helper), assistants
(as in administrative assistant), or associates (as in research associate) without ever advancing to head of the laboratory, manager
of the office, or principal member of the research staff.

When men are expected to behave in a stereotypical manner—to automatically assume the leader's role in a mixed-sex
group, pay for a business lunch with a female colleague, or con-
front a poorly performing colleague—sex role spillover also
occurs.

Although many aspects of gender roles can carry over to
work, the sex object aspect is the most relevant to the topic of sex
at work. Being a sex object is one aspect of the female sex role,
perhaps a fairly central aspect, but it is not clear whether there
is a comparably strong sexual aspect to the male sex role. If there
is, it probably concerns sexual aggressiveness or assertiveness. In
any event, the carryover of the sexual aspects of sex roles into the
workplace, the aspect of sex role spillover emphasized by Gutek
and Morasch (1982), is likely to be related to sexuality at work.

The sex role spillover explanation is an outgrowth of role
theory. More specifically, it depends on the concepts of work role
and sex role. A *work role* is a set of expectations associated with
the tasks to be accomplished on a job (Katz and Kahn, 1978). The
expectations are shared: A secretary has a set of expectations
about what is appropriate behavior for a secretary, and other people in the organization also have expectations about what constitutes appropriate secretarial behavior. Since each employee
occupies an organizational role, an organization can be viewed as
a set of role relationships (Katz and Kahn, 1978). Katz and Kahn
cited Floyd Allport's concept, partial inclusion, to depict the notion that organizations do not want "whole people." Organizations
want role occupants. Hypothetically, work role behavior is identical across people who occupy the same role. In practice, work
roles are usually tailored to some degree by the worker, to fit his
or her own personality and self-concept. Nevertheless, some as-

pects of the self are considered inappropriate to work roles. Excessive expression of emotions, for example, is usually inappropriate to a work role, unless perhaps one is a performing artist—a conductor or actor. Likewise, sexuality is a part of the self that is generally considered inappropriate to work roles. If people at work behaved within the narrow confines of work roles, then sexual jokes, flirtatious behavior, sexual overtures, and sexual coercion would not exist in most workplaces.

If the work role is a set of shared expectations about behavior in a job, the sex role is a set of shared expectations about the behavior of women and men. Sex role expectations are carried over into the workplace for at least three reasons. One is that gender identity seems to be a more basic cognitive category than work role (Bem, 1981; Laws, 1979). Bem noted that the prevalence of gender-based cognitive processing—thinking about people as men or women—stems in part from society's insistence that an individual's sex makes a difference in "virtually every domain of human experience." Thus, a person is often categorized as a man or woman first, a nurse or pipefitter second. Further, a male pipefitter may be evaluated quite differently than a female pipefitter (Nilson, 1976). To realize the salience of gender as a basis for categorizing people, try to remember the last time you met someone whose gender you cannot recall. The list of such people is likely to be short. Contrast that with the last time you met a person whose occupation you knew but cannot now recall. Under most circumstances, gender is the single most salient social characteristic. We notice people's gender and remember it long after we have forgotten their other characteristics. Thus, the characteristics we associate with gender, sex role expectations, are likely to be salient at work as in other settings.

A second reason why sex role may spill over into work role is that women may feel more comfortable with stereotypically female roles in some circumstances, particularly if they feel that men at work will only accept them in a "female" role. Kanter (1977a) identified three traditionally female roles that women may choose, or be forced to adopt, because such roles seem to make everyone more comfortable: pet, mother, and sex object.

The women a man most frequently interacts with are likely

to be a spouse or date, his own daughters, or his own mother. Thus, in interaction with women, a man's role is most often that of spouse, lover, parent, or child, and men may feel more comfortable falling back on these more familiar role relationships (Nieva and Gutek, 1981). When confronting a female engineer for the first time in his life, a male engineer may treat her like his mother (if that is the image he has of her) or as a sex object (if she seems an appropriate target) because those styles of interacting with women are familiar, and comfortable, to him.

Sex role spillover facilitates the expression of sexuality at work to the extent that the sex object aspect of the female sex role and the sexual aggressor aspect of the male sex role carry over into the work setting. This appears to be the case in particular when men and women work together or at least come into contact with opposite-sex employees in the course of their work.

The sex role spillover perspective combines some of the aspects of the organizational and sociocultural models as proposed by Tangri, Burt, and Johnson (1982) as explanations for sexual harassment. It also combines aspects of three explanations described by Nieva and Gutek (1981): the structural institutional explanation for women's status at work, the sex role explanation, and the intergroup explanation. Sex role spillover focuses on the workplace and its environment rather than on either individual differences or broad cultural themes. One advantage of focusing on the workplace is that it can serve as an arena for handling problems explicated by the intergroup and sex role models. The workplace may be a more manageable arena for change than society at large.

Implications for Managers and Others

As mentioned earlier, we know relatively little about the topic of sex in the workplace; it is there waiting to be studied. The topic, however, is worth studying for many reasons. To simply describe and interpret the phenomenon without specifying the implications for organizations and management would be a shame since sex discrimination and sexual harassment loom so large among current organizational problems.

Sex discrimination cases including sexual harassment have been increasing steadily. At present, they constitute the largest group of employees' complaints to California's Department of Fair Employment and Housing. The Equal Employment Opportunity Commission shows the same trend. In response to the increasing number of complaints, increasingly strong laws have been passed to encourage employers to eliminate sexual harassment. These new laws are typified by California's Senate Bill 2012, which went into effect January 1, 1985. This bill makes it an unlawful employment practice to fail to take reasonable steps to prevent sexual harassment. Most large organizations have already been subject to multiple lawsuits in this area. In addition to the cost of court cases, which is painfully obvious to management, our research shows other costs to organizations in the form of lower productivity, less efficiency, and lower job satisfaction, as well as loss of valuable employees through resignation, voluntary transfer to other departments, and lowered commitment to the organization.

To formulate training programs, set up procedures for handling a problem, and deal with formal complaints without understanding the underlying issue puts one at a distinct disadvantage. That is the difficult position of many human resources specialists in organizations today. Although knowing the laws and regulations regarding sexual harassment and sex discrimination is important, many managers, consultants, and training specialists who know the law probably do not understand the phenomenon of sex in the workplace.

The first goal of the following chapters, then, is to use this research project to describe and interpret sex in the workplace, both problematic sex and whatever other sexual activity there is at work. Another important goal, however, is to specify implications for women and men and organizations of all the findings and ultimately to make some recommendations and specify actions that organizations can take. My research and consulting over the past six years lead to the following strong conviction: sex in the workplace today is a problem for many organizations in overt and covert ways, but it is not particularly resistant to change or difficult to solve if management wants to eliminate it.

Research Design

The foremost concern of the research project was in establishing base rates of various forms of heterosexual social-sexual behavior at work, with a special emphasis on learning the extent of sexual harassment. I wanted to study sexuality at work as an example of organizational behavior; I also wanted to emphasize those aspects of the work environment that affect sex at work. I was further interested in examining various explanations for the existence of social-sexual behavior, most notably the sex role spillover perspective.

Although I recognize that not all sexuality or sexual harassment is heterosexual, I decided to limit the study to the interaction between men and women and the interaction of work roles and sex roles. Homosexual harassment, especially men harassing men, also happens, as my own preliminary studies and other research indicate (U.S. Merit Systems Protection Board, 1981). Some of my findings can be generalized from heterosexual to homosexual experiences.

A representative survey of working women and men in Los Angeles County, interviewed by telephone in their homes, was selected as the method of study. As one of the geographically largest counties in the United States, Los Angeles County provides a large, diverse sample of working people, mostly urban workers.

The Field Research Corporation of San Francisco was awarded a subcontract to conduct telephone interviews with 800 adult working women and 400 adult working men, randomly selected. All working people living in households with telephones in Los Angeles County were eligible for inclusion. Women were oversampled because most of the reports of sexual harassment concern female victims, and women have been most vocal about the negative effects of sexuality at work. The final sample consisted of 827 women and 405 men, all eighteen or older, employed outside the home twenty hours a week or more, and regularly in contact with members of the opposite sex at work as coworkers, supervisors, customers, or clients.

More detailed background on the study, including selection

of the method of data collection, is in Appendix A. The sampling procedures are described in Appendix B, and Appendix C provides the set of questions used in the interview schedule.

Some of the respondents were called again as part of a dissertation by Jensen (1981). The 293 women who reported more serious forms of social-sexual behavior were called again fourteen to sixteen months after the initial contact; they constitute the follow-up sample. The sampling procedures for the follow-up study are described in Appendix B and in Jensen (1981); the questionnaire is available in Jensen.

Now, let us turn to the results. Before examining people's experiences with sex at work in Chapters Three and Four, I consider the work environment of men and women in Chapter Two. The workplace, the stage on which all the action occurs, shapes and influences the actors' behavior.

TWO

The Workplace:
A Setting
for Sexual Behavior

Understanding the work environment is crucial to understanding what occurs there. Sexual behavior at work takes place in an organization having its own culture, its own norms and regulations, a hierarchy of job classifications, and diverse tasks carried out by a variety of people. While organizations differ along these dimensions—some have a rigid hierarchy while others have fewer formal levels of command or are organized along a matrix—other aspects are relatively similar across companies. For example, people are more likely to think of an affair as taking place between a male manager and a female secretary than between a female manager and a male secretary because women tend to work as secretaries, men as managers. This is true in all kinds of organizations—hierarchical and nonhierarchical, for example. Men and women are not randomly distributed throughout organizations. Explaining how men's and women's jobs differ shows how sex role spillover operates and provides a context for understanding the nature of social-sexual experiences between the sexes.

Characteristics of Work Environments

My research identified four aspects of the work environment that are important for understanding sex in the workplace.

Table 1. Relationship of Sex of Respondent
to Occupation Classification.

	Men (N = 401)	Women (N = 823)
Professional	25.7%	24.8%
Managerial	16.5	8.0
Clerical	17.8	46.9
Skilled	14.6	2.4
Semiskilled	13.8	6.9
Unskilled	3.0	0.5
Service workers	7.7	10.5
	100.0%	100.0%

Note: Percentages rounded.

The first is the sex segregation of work. That work is sex segregated is widely known (see Nieva and Gutek, 1981; Lipman-Blumen, 1984), yet its importance to sexuality has not been recognized. The second aspect is the difference in status, prestige, and power of men and women at work. Third is the nature of the working conditions. And fourth is the extent to which some personal characteristics of job holders such as physical attractiveness are emphasized on the job. All four of these aspects of the work environment reflect sex role spillover.

Sex Segregation of Work. The sex segregated nature of the labor force has been widely documented (Nieva and Gutek, 1981). Women predominate in only a few traditionally female jobs; for example, about 42 percent of employed women aged twenty to twenty-four were in clerical work in 1977 (Barrett, 1979). Laws (1979) noted that in 1970, jobs were so sex segregated that 69 percent of men (or women) would have to change occupations to eliminate sex segregation of work. In the past ten years, the situation has remained essentially the same (Jacobs, 1983).

People in the Los Angeles study also work in sex segregated occupations. Table 1 shows the distribution of men and women in the study across major occupational groups. Women have less diversity than men. Almost three fourths of the women are in just two occupational categories: clerical and professional. Within the professional job category, women are clustered in such traditionally female fields as teaching and nursing. Women are most underrepresented in skilled blue-collar jobs.

These findings suggest that the percentage of young women in clerical jobs may be increasing, a trend that has gone unnoticed by the media interested in women's entry into blue-collar jobs and male-dominated professions. Whereas 42 percent of American women aged twenty to twenty-four were in clerical jobs in 1977, 57 percent of Los Angeles women aged twenty to twenty-four were in clerical jobs in 1980. Not surprisingly, teenage women in Los Angeles in 1980 were even more likely to work in clerical jobs. Sixty-three percent of working women under age twenty were in clerical jobs, whereas 44 percent of women over twenty-four were in clerical jobs. Overall, 47 percent of working women in Los Angeles County held clerical jobs in 1980.

The survey directly demonstrated the degree of sex segregation of working people in Los Angeles County (shown in Figure 1). Each person's occupation was coded using the three-digit U.S. Bureau of the Census codes. Because the bureau publishes the number of women and men in each occupation, we were able to compute the percentage of females in each three-digit occupational category. (The 1980 Bureau of the Census figures were not yet available when these analyses were performed. Staines, Pleck, Shepard, and O'Connor (1978) used this procedure.) Figure 1 shows the distribution of women and men in the sample across the percentage of females in an occupation. In a completely sex integrated occupational world, 20 percent of men and women would be found in each category of "percent female in occupation." Figure 1 shows a sex segregated occupational world where 61.8 percent of the men in the Los Angeles County sample worked in occupations that were overwhelmingly male—that is, fewer than 20 percent of the people in the occupation were women, according to 1970 census figures. Eighteen percent of the women in the sample worked in male-dominated occupations, occupations with fewer than 20 percent female workers.

A smaller proportion of workers were in female-dominated jobs; 40.3 percent of women and just 4.7 percent of men surveyed in 1980 were in occupations that in 1970 were strongly female

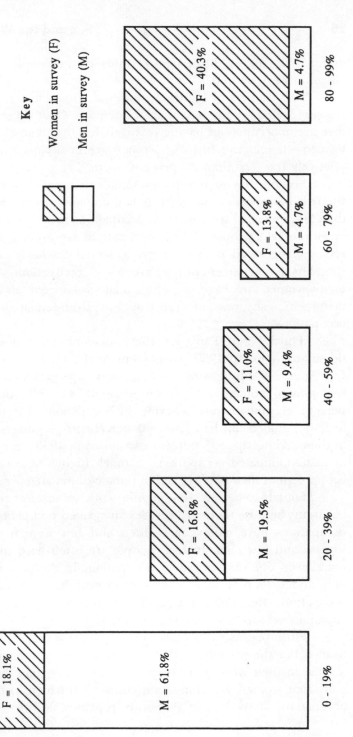

Figure 1. Distribution of Men and Women in the Survey by the Sex Ratio of Their Occupation.

dominated—that is, 80 percent or more of the people in the occupation were women.

Five features of Figure 1 stand out. First, more men are in
sex segregated occupations than women are. Over three fifths of
men are in occupations having relatively few (less than 20 percent)
women whereas two fifths of women are in occupations having
relatively few (less than 20 percent) men.

Second, few men work in female-dominated occupations,
whereas more women work in male-dominated occupations. Less
than 20 percent of men work in occupations in which 40 percent
or more of the people in those occupations are women. Male secretaries, registered nurses, or grade school teachers are indeed
rare; less than 5 percent of men are in such occupations. Although
many women are eager to enter male-dominated occupations,
men seem to shy away, or even run away, from female-dominated
occupations.

Third, Figure 1 suggests that women are moving into male-
dominated jobs. In 1980, 18 percent of the women surveyed in
Los Angeles County were working in occupations whose repre-
sentation of women in 1970 was under 20 percent. Another 17
percent of women were working in occupations that were also
male-dominated but had from 20 percent to 39 percent women
in them. Altogether, 35 percent of women in 1980 were working
in male-dominated occupations, a much higher figure than the
9.4 percent of men who worked in female-dominated occupations.

Fourth, relatively few people work in sex integrated occupations because there are few sex integrated occupations. Most
occupations have either many men and few women or many
women and few men. In fact, people are often hard pressed to
name even one sex integrated occupation. In the present study,
only about 10 percent of each sex worked in a sex integrated
occupation. (Real estate sales and clinical psychology are two occupations relatively sex integrated today.)

Fifth, because men work in more sex segregated work than
women do, the probability that they will come into contact with
women in their work is relatively low and lower than the probability that women will come into contact with men in the same
occupation. Many men in the study probably do not work with

Table 2. Relationship of Sex of Respondent to Sex Ratio of Job.

	Men (N = 385)	Women (N = 784)
More men than women in job	72.2%	19.6%
Equal number of men and women in job	16.6	20.9
More women than men in job	11.2	59.4
	100.0%	100.0%

Note: Percentages rounded.

any women in their own occupation, and some may not even know any women in their occupation. This "femaleless" occupational world that many men experience is bound to affect their interactions with women at work and their attitudes about women generally. One man in the survey reported that he had never met a working woman who was not interested in a "free meal." This man works in a male-dominated occupation, and it is probably safe to guess that he has never had a female supervisor.

Such issues about contact with the opposite sex at work can better be explored with more direct questions about the work situation than they can using U.S. Bureau of the Census occupational codes. Yet figures on the sex segregation of the labor force are often obtained from census data that lack information about day-to-day behavior on the job. Although such information is not obtainable in census data, large sections of our questionnaire were devoted to questions about the current workplace and contact with the opposite sex at work. The survey was particularly interested in sex segregation on the job as contrasted with sex segregation of occupation. I defined a *job* as an occupation within a particular workplace. For example, engineering is an occupation, but engineers work at specific jobs in company A making weapons systems or in company B making computers or in company C supplying electricity. Common sense, personal experience, and anecdotal evidence (Wallace, 1976, cited in Laws, 1979) suggest that sex segregation may be greater within jobs than within occupations. For example, although waiting tables is a female-dominated occupation, some restaurants hire only waiters, others only waitresses.

Table 2 shows some similarities between sex segregation of

occupation and job. For example, more men than women are in sex segregated jobs. Over 72 percent of the men report that on their jobs there are more men than women. Once again, women reported that most of their coworkers on the same job were women. And again, women were more likely than men to work in jobs dominated by the opposite sex.

Sex segregation of occupation and sex segregation of job are related, of course. Seventy-four percent of women who work in an extremely female-dominated occupation also work with more women on their jobs. But 42 percent of the women who work in extremely male-dominated occupations still work with more women on their jobs in their own companies, providing support for the contention that jobs may be sex segregated within an organization, sometimes in the opposite direction from the occupation as a whole. For example, one organization may hire only female mechanics; three female attorneys may open a law office together; the personnel department in a women's clothing store may be all female. Thus, women in some nontraditional occupations may still work with all women. This job sex segregation (in contrast to occupational sex segregation) can help to explain why women and men in the same occupational categories have different incomes. For example, a female-dominated personnel department may have a lower wage scale than a male-dominated personnel department.

Other, more subtle measures of sex segregation in the study include occupational choice. The extent to which occupations are presented as more appropriate or suitable to one sex than the other is an indirect measure of sex segregation of work. Several research studies show that women have a more restricted choice of occupations readily available to them than men have (see Nieva and Gutek, 1981; Siegel, 1973; Oppenheimer, 1968). That is, relatively few jobs are labeled "women's jobs" in comparison to the relatively large and diverse set of "men's jobs."

This discrepancy is illustrated by comparing the women in the study employed in women's work (occupation and job in which the majority of workers are women) with the women in the study employed in men's work (occupation and job in which the majority of workers are men). About 11 percent of the women in the study work in men's occupations and men's jobs whereas about 30 percent are in women's occupations and women's jobs. The number of job titles held by the 11 percent of women in men's work far exceeds the number of job titles held by the 30 percent of women in women's work—fifty-three different job titles to thirty-eight, to be exact. Among the fifty-three different job titles held by women in men's work, only a few are considered clerical (such as vehicle dispatcher, computer operator, and stock clerk) whereas 35 percent are technical and professional occupations such as accountant, architect, chemical engineer, draftsperson, and photographer. Among the blue-collar and service jobs held by these women are upholsterer, bus driver, sheriff-bailiff, bartender, and furnace-smelter operator. Clearly, occupations numerically dominated by men have variety.

In contrast, many fewer job titles—thirty-eight—were held by the larger group of women, the 30 percent who worked in female-dominated occupations and jobs. A full 55 percent of those job titles are clerical and almost half are in a single job classification—secretary. Other clerical jobs held by the women in the study include bank teller, bookkeeper, file clerk, receptionist, and telephone operator. Only seven technical and professional jobs are represented, including registered nurse, clinical lab technician, dental hygienist, and elementary school teacher. Only one blue-collar job is represented (sewer-stitcher), while the various service jobs include waitress, health aide, flight attendant, hairdresser, and housekeeper.

As measured here, men's work is more diverse than women's work, includes a greater number of job titles, and is distinct from women's work (see also Oppenheimer, 1968). No wonder women are eager to enter men's jobs. Among other advantages, men's work offers more varied possibilities. Women's work by contrast not only pays less but also provides relatively few new or exciting options for men. (Salary differences are not covered in this study but are well documented elsewhere; see Rosenbaum, 1985; Treiman and Hartmann, 1981; Madden, 1985; Blau, 1977.) Few of these women's jobs offer great opportunities for advancement, and hardly any can be considered glamorous, with flight attendant (formerly airline stewardess) as a possible exception.

Other indirect measures of sex segregation at work were included in the questionnaire, and their results corroborate the findings already reported. For example, both sexes thought it would be harder for the opposite sex than for the same sex to get their job, but they agreed that it is harder for women to get the jobs held by men than it is for men to get the jobs held by women. For example, 42 percent of the men in the study admitted that it would be harder for a woman than for a man to get their job. In contrast, only 23 percent of the women said it would be harder for a man than for a woman to get their job. Although it is apparently relatively easy for men to get women's jobs, they are not doing so, whereas women, who have a harder time getting men's jobs, are doing so, as Figure 1 suggested.

Several other questions measured contact with the opposite sex at work, as yet another indirect measure of sex segregation. Men and women reported that they were equally likely to talk to the other sex about social matters, but women were more likely than men to talk about job-related matters with the other sex and were much more likely to work with men than men were to work with women. These findings add evidence to the contention that men are more isolated from women in their work than women are from men. Some men interact with some women socially at work more than they interact with them in work-related matters.

An analysis of the relationship among the various sex segregation measures revealed that the amount of job-related talk or social talk with the other sex was not strongly related to the percentage of females in the occupation or job. Thus, interaction between the sexes seems not to be impeded by the sex ratio of jobs. Even people who work in sex segregated jobs tend to talk with the other sex at work. They do not work in a one-sex environment, just a one-sex job. This relatively high level of communication between the sexes at work may help to obscure the extent to which jobs are sex segregated.

In summary, jobs within organizations are sex segregated to an even greater extent than is apparent by examining just the sex composition of occupational categories. The reality of the extreme sex segregation of jobs may be masked somewhat by the relatively great amount of interaction—both work related and purely social—between the sexes at work.

Despite the fact that men, compared to women, report that they would have less difficulty entering nontraditional jobs, men apparently have relatively little interest in doing so. My findings are consistent with Schreiber's (1979) research showing that men entering female-dominated clerical jobs did not anticipate (or encounter) hostility from women in these jobs. Furthermore, the men in Schreiber's study expected that it would be easy to learn their new jobs and they expected to advance rapidly. Despite these advantages, Jacobs (1983) reported that men who move into women's occupations also tend to change occupations again, back to male-dominated jobs.

Status and Hierarchy. Men dominate the highest-status jobs. The present study included four measures that reflect status or hierarchy: prestige of job, income, supervising others, and being supervised by others. In general, jobs that are considered high in prestige, pay well, involve supervision of others, and are themselves free from close supervision will be higher in status and farther up the hierarchy than other jobs. In our survey, compared to female workers, male workers reported significantly higher-prestige jobs; 47 percent of the men and 33 percent of the women said their jobs were high in prestige. Men were also more likely than women to supervise the work of others. Almost 61 percent of the men said they supervised others, compared to 41 percent of the women. On the other hand, women were more likely to report that they have a supervisor; 86 percent of the women and 76 percent of the men said they have a supervisor at work.

With respect to income, male workers report higher family incomes than female workers, although female workers are more likely than male workers to have a working spouse. For example, 7 percent of the men but 13 percent of the women reported a family income of $10 thousand a year or less. Thus, although the female worker's family income is likely to include a male worker, it is still significantly lower than the male worker's family income. This measure of family income is a very conservative measure of status of the worker, but it is consistent with other findings. In general, men report higher-status jobs and higher family incomes. Although the findings on status are not as dramatic as the findings on sex segregation, they do suggest that men's and women's jobs differ on that dimension.

Working Conditions. Another area where men's and women's jobs are reported to differ is in working conditions (Crowley, Levitin, and Quinn, 1973; Nieva and Gutek, 1981). According to Herzberg, Mausner, and Snyderman (1959), women value such factors as pleasant, clean surroundings more than men do. After reviewing the scant literature on the topic, Nieva and Gutek (1981) concluded that women, on the average, do have more comfortable, clean work environments than men do (see also Quinn and Shepard, 1974).

Our survey also suggests that women are more likely than men to work in clean, comfortable surroundings. For example, women, more often than men, are in white-collar jobs where the work environment is usually clean and attractive, with a comfortable temperature and adequate lighting. Eighty percent of the women and 61 percent of the men in the study are white-collar workers: professionals, managers, clerks, secretaries, and salespeople. Women also work in environments with less swearing or sexual jokes, and they report that they are less often treated disrespectfully than men are. Although what constitutes obscene language or disrespectful treatment is highly subjective and varies greatly from person to person, the differences reported by men and women are telling. Almost half of the women but 38 percent of the men said they were never treated disrespectfully at work. Twenty-six percent of the men but only 14 percent of the women reported that swearing and obscene language were heard frequently in their work environment; 31 percent of the men but only 24 percent of the women said that sexual joking and talking occurred frequently.

Disrespectful treatment, swearing, and sexual talk and jokes may characterize interaction among men but not among women; these results may simply reflect the sex segregated nature of work. Taken together, however, they provide support for the contention that pleasant working conditions are associated with women's work more than men's work.

Personality and Personal Appearance. Researchers interested in characteristics of jobs have rarely considered the possibility that personal appearance or personality might be important in a job although popular books on "getting ahead" often stress the importance of personal appearance (Molloy, 1975, 1977). Substantial research findings in social psychology show that various positive characteristics are attributed to attractive people (Berscheid and Walster, 1974; Cash, Kehr, Polyson, and Freeman, 1977; Dion, Berscheid, and Walster, 1972). For example, attractive people are viewed as more popular, a finding that is not surprising, but they are also viewed as more moral—better people. Since we know that personal appearance affects the way people are treated everywhere—in school, in restaurants, in stores—it makes sense that it is important at work. Unfortunately, physical attributes rarely have been examined in the context of work, except in hiring decisions.

In our survey, over half of working women said that physical attractiveness and a "good" personality were at least somewhat important in their jobs, especially with respect to treatment accorded them by the other sex. Almost 20 percent of the women and over 10 percent of the men said physical attractiveness was very important on their jobs. Having a good personality was even more important than physical attractiveness, according to 40 percent of the surveyed men and almost 60 percent of the women, who said personality was very important in how they were treated by the other sex at work. Although attractiveness is important for everyone, it is more important for women than men.

In general, the measures of the importance of physical attractiveness were not strongly related, but if people were influenced by an opposite-sex colleague's personality, they were also influenced by that person's physical attractiveness. This makes sense, of course. The jobs in which personal appearance counts, for example, receptionist, flight attendant, waitress, or sales manager, also require personable behavior or "a good personality." Other jobs, for example, truck driver, computer programmer, or sewing-machine operator, do not require either. In addition, the relationship between the importance of physical attractiveness on the job and in treatment by the opposite sex was stronger for women than for men; that is, when women said that physical appearance was an important part of the job, they also said that their physical appearance affected the way men treated them. This was not necessarily true for men. Even if the job required physical attractiveness, the women at work did not necessarily respond to them according to their level of attractiveness. The relationship between the importance of physical attractiveness on the job and in treatment by the opposite sex was stronger for women than men, possibly because men are a more important part of women's jobs (both in terms of amount of contact and in likelihood that the supervisor is male) than women are of men's jobs.

Predicting a Worker's Gender

All four aspects of the work environment that were studied—sex segregation, status and hierarchy, working conditions, and personality and personal characteristics—were used to predict a worker's gender. The analyses addressed the following question: Given the clear differences in the way the two sexes describe their work environments, are those differences large enough to predict a worker's sex on the basis of their answers to those questions? The strategy employed was to see first if all the items together could successfully discriminate male from female workers. If they could discriminate working men from women, could some subset of the questions predict a worker's sex equally well? Finally, which of the four aspects of the work environment are best at predicting a worker's sex? I used a discriminant analysis program that attempts to classify all workers into the two categories of female and male.

A preliminary discriminant analysis using the measures of segregation, status, working conditions, and personal appearance resulted in 82 percent of the people—88 percent of the women and 69 percent of the men—being correctly classified by sex. Additional analyses showed it is possible to eliminate many of the predictors without losing predictive power. Nine of the original eighteen measures of the work environment correctly classified 80 percent of the workers, 83 percent of the men and 79 percent of the women.

The results show that the answer to our first question is yes, it is possible to predict a worker's sex on the basis of responses about work. In general, compared to men, more women hold white-collar jobs, where most employees in the occupation and job in the person's organization are women. Their jobs are low in prestige and lack supervisory responsibility. Finally, physical attractiveness and having a pleasing personality are important on the job and affect the way men at work treat them.

To find out how well each of the four areas was able to predict a worker's sex, four separate analyses were run. Of the four areas, sex segregation is the strongest predictor of a worker's sex. Eighty-three percent of the men were correctly classified as men by the analysis, and 79 percent of the women were correctly classified as women on the basis of four measures of sex segregation. These sex segregation measures correctly classified as many people as the more extensive analyses, suggesting that the other three classes of variables—status and hierarchy, working conditions, and personal characteristics—add little in predictive power over and above the measures of sex segregation.

Separate analyses of the other three areas confirm this conclusion. Status and hierarchy alone were not able to effectively discriminate between male and female workers. They correctly classified workers by sex at a level only slightly better than chance. Working conditions fared only slightly better, and the five questions concerning personality and personal appearance together correctly classified 59 percent of the women and 69 percent of the men.

Although the results clearly show that men and women work in different kinds of environments, fine distinctions cannot be made about the relative importance of the four kinds of measures because they are not all measured equally validly or reliably. The survey was not designed specifically to test the relative ability of these measures to discriminate female from male workers.

To summarize, the most important difference between male and female work is a scarcity of other-sex workers; men work in a more gender homogeneous environment than women do. This sex segregation of work facilitates the occurrence of sex role spillover. When some jobs are done by men but not by women, it is easy to infuse those jobs with the characteristics of the male sex role and vice versa—jobs requiring characteristics associated with the male sex role are more likely to be open to men but closed to women.

Other differences between women's and men's work appear to be outcomes or concomitants of sex segregation. Three important outcomes or concomitants of sex segregation were identified and are consistent with the sex role spillover perspective. Each corresponds to one of the different "control myths" identified by Lipman-Blumen (1984). She uses *control myths* to describe beliefs about men or women that preserve the existing power differential between the sexes.

One outcome of sex segregation is that, consistent with the general stereotype of male competence and leadership, men occupy higher-status positions than women do. A second outcome, consistent with the general stereotype of women being more delicate but also "nicer" and less aggressive, is that women tend to have somewhat more pleasant working conditions than men do. A third outcome, consistent with the role of women as sex objects, is a greater emphasis in women's than in men's jobs on being personable and physically attractive.

The first two of these outcomes, concerning status and working conditions, are frequently included in the research of organizational psychologists, but the third, about the importance of personal appearance and personality, is not. However, this outcome is consistent with Lipman-Blumen's (1984) sixth control myth, the notion that beauty and sexuality are women's most valuable assets. She calls it the "big beauty and sexuality buy-off," which works as follows: "Women, they are told, are more beautiful, more delicate, more moral, more understanding and humane than men. They should be happy that they do not have to get dirty, wear plain clothes, fight and compete for wages. This message induces both women and men to overemphasize and overvalue female beauty" (Lipman-Blumen, 1984, p. 89).

No wonder women in women's jobs are expected to be as personable and attractive at work as they are elsewhere—a striking example of sex role spillover. Why this factor has not been identified in organizational research is not entirely clear. Perhaps a lack of research on women workers or an emphasis on studying and confirming the rationality of work organizations has contributed to the relative neglect of the importance of physical appearance and personable behavior at work.

Influence of Sex of Supervisor on the Work Environment

Supervisor, boss, manager, department head, foreman—a worker's immediate superior, however labeled, has a great deal of influence over a worker's behavior both directly and indirectly in the kind of environment he or she creates for workers. One's direct superior reviews performance, may determine pay and rate of advancement, and is considered the appropriate person with whom to lodge complaints. The direct superior is usually the single most important organizational member for any worker.

Fourteen percent of women and a significantly larger percentage of men, 24 percent, have no supervisor. Almost all of the men (92 percent) and over half of the women have male supervisors. Only 9 percent of the men who have male supervisors work in occupations in which at least half of the workers are female. Not surprisingly, for both sexes, workers with female supervisors are more likely than those with male supervisors to be in female-dominated occupations. Women tend to supervise all-female groups.

Sex of supervisor is also related to contact with the opposite sex at work. Not surprisingly, for both sexes, having an opposite-sex supervisor means spending more work time and having more work-related discussions with the opposite sex. The fact that so few men have female supervisors closes one kind of contact with women at work. Employees necessarily need a certain level of contact with a supervisor, whereas they may be able to avoid some colleagues. For example, a male engineer may ignore a new female engineer if she is a coworker but not if she is his superior. However, the survey's results suggest that the probability of a female engineer being appointed as supervisor over a group of male engineers is very low indeed.

Why do so few men have female supervisors? One explanation is tied to the sex segregation of jobs. If men and women are in different jobs, then they could be expected to have same-sex supervisors. Yet, over half the women workers have male supervisors. Clearly, other factors are operating.

One common explanation is that men do not like to work for women, the assumption being that it is somehow inappropriate for men to take orders from women or that women would not be good supervisors. The obverse of this is that men are particularly competent and capable supervisors, that leadership is a masculine trait. Recently, several observers (Kanter, 1977a; Nieva and Gutek, 1981) have suggested that if men are dissatisfied with a female supervisor, it is because she has low status and little power in the organization. Our study of Los Angeles County workers supports this interpretation. The men who work for women do report lower job satisfaction than other men, but that lower job satisfaction can be explained by their low wages and the low prestige of their jobs. The few men who have prestigious jobs and work for women do not report lower job satisfaction. Most of the men who work for women, however, are in low-status, low-paying office jobs because that is where women are supervisors. Their dissatisfaction with the job, however, seems to be related more to the job than to the gender of the supervisor.

An interesting related finding of our survey is that men with female supervisors apparently feel not only that their female supervisors have little power or influence in the organization but also that their supervisors have little control over them. This may reflect their feeling that it is inappropriate for a woman to supervise a man.

Some research literature suggests that women do not like working for a female supervisor (Petty and Miles, 1976). Although the research on women workers' reactions to female supervisors is sketchy, the research on beliefs about women's reactions to women bosses is clearer. Men in particular think women prefer male supervisors (Bass, Krusall, and Alexander, 1971). In this survey, there was no difference in job satisfaction between women who had male versus female supervisors.

Summary

A tour of almost any firm graphically illustrates the main point of this chapter: Work is sex segregated. The payroll department consists of a group of young women and their male supervisor. The word processing department is also a group of women, this time with a female supervisor promoted from the ranks. The quality assurance department is a group of men with a male supervisor. Even the factory floor is highly sex segregated, the women performing the assembly of small parts under a male foreman, the men working in shipping and receiving. In another organization, some of the same tasks may be assigned to the other sex. Many factors contribute to the segregation of men and women at work, but what is so consistent across organizations— and so psychologically important—is the extent to which jobs are performed by one sex only.

This situation can evoke two responses. The most common one is probably to assume that the organization of work into male and female spheres is natural and normal, reflecting some innate differences between men and women. Women are somehow more suited to answering the telephone, assembling electronics, and keying in text while men are suited to leading in all situations, cataloguing parts, drafting plans, and repairing plumbing. In fact, this sex segregation may seem so natural that it is not even consciously considered. (A manager once described his department of eight engineers and two secretaries to me as "eight guys and two girls.")

A less common reaction is one of awe at the incredible power of social institutions to shape people's behavior. Why do from one third to one half of all women end up doing clerical and secretarial work? A much smaller proportion of women express an interest in doing that work. Women's college majors and programs also reflect much more diversity (Jacobs, 1985). Why should work be more sex segregated than higher education? If equally qualified individuals were more or less randomly hired for equally good jobs, a woman with a history or psychology major would be as likely as a man to get a personnel job in an aerospace firm. Yet a man is likely to end up in that job and a woman in a more traditional area.

Recently the sex segregation of work has been the subject of much research and controversy, mostly centering around its role in women's lower wages. The more general point of much of this research is that sex segregation is not so much an outgrowth of natural male and female traits as it is a mechanism that leads to certain effects, low wages being a prime example. Sex segregation is a cause, not just an effect.

I contend that sex segregation of work facilitates sex role spillover because segregating work by sex calls attention to gender. As discussed in Chapter One, gender is the single most noticeable, salient aspect of people. The segregation of work into men's work and women's work encourages sex role spillover, the assumption that people in particular jobs and the jobs themselves have characteristics of one gender. Thus, if one asks why a particular electronics assembly is done by men, the answer may be that the job requires mechanical aptitude and good spatial relations. The same assembly task done by women in another plant is explained on the basis of women's patience and ability to handle detail work. I contend that, to some extent, the choice of male or female workers comes first, and the explanation or justification afterward.

There is substantial pressure to continue sex segregation of jobs, despite government attempts to open various jobs to women. The workers in the survey reported that it is harder for women to get men's jobs than vice versa. It is difficult for women to get into leadership positions, especially in male-dominated jobs, although neither sex evaluates female supervisors more negatively than male supervisors, other things being equal. Managers need to be aware of the pressures toward sex segregation. In particular, they need to know that despite any government regulations and their company's own attempts to integrate jobs, women are not especially welcome by their new colleagues in nontraditional jobs. Whether the new job is public relations manager, head of data processing, stock handler, or millwright, the men in those fields readily admit that men do not particularly welcome women on the job.

Despite these pressures to maintain sex segregation, women are entering fields dominated by men. About 35 percent of working women in 1980 were in occupations that in 1970 were clearly male dominated. This suggests some small step toward sex integration of work and indicates that the various programs and attempts to integrate work are having an effect.

Given some degree of resistance or hostility by male co-workers, it is not surprising that even as women move into non-traditional occupations, they may find themselves with female, not male, colleagues. Many women in this survey who work in non-traditional occupations work primarily with women either by their own choice to work with women or, more often, out of an interest in finding a pleasant, cooperative work environment. If women feel isolated or ostracized in male-dominated environments, they will gravitate toward workplaces with more women, if they can find them. The result of these various pressures is that jobs are more sex segregated than occupations.

Men are more often sex segregated at work than women. Relatively few men interact with women as colleagues or supervisors at work. Men's contact with women is not only often limited to social talk or supervision in work-related matters but also such women probably work in jobs low in prestige and income. Furthermore, many of those women work in jobs where having an attractive physical appearance or attractive personality is important.

A picture emerges of a work environment where an attractive appearance and personality are valued for women and where men socialize with subordinate women who are attractive and personable and hold low-paying, low-prestige jobs, usually clerical. That this situation seems natural and normal for so many people is testimony to the power of sex roles in shaping our view of the work world. Such a situation where sex role spillover occurs sets up the conditions for the expression of sexuality, including sexual harassment, to which we now turn.

THREE

Sexual Harassment:
Nature and Frequency

Because so much attention has centered on sexual harassment and because it is a problem for individuals and organizations, Chapters Three and Four focus on its scope and magnitude. How common is sex at work? How much of it could be considered sexual harassment: 90 percent, 50 percent, 10 percent? My research method, a random-sample survey of working people, is ideally suited to learning the scope and magnitude of sex and sexual harassment at work, who is harassed, and who does the harassing.

This chapter and the following establish some base rates for sex and harassment at work and examine the targets of overtures and harassment, the initiators of sexual interchanges, and the reactions of harassment victims. Chapter Three describes the extent of harassment and other kinds of sexual behavior at work and the targets of sexual overtures. Chapter Four discusses the harassers and the reactions of victims of harassment.

The objective of this study was to examine sexuality in the more general context of organizational behavior and sex role spillover. An operating assumption at the beginning was that the experiences of sexuality at work, including sexual harassment, are subjective. It would be difficult, if not impossible, to make a comprehensive list of events that are necessarily experienced as sexual harassment. Furthermore, at the time of the survey, final legal guidelines about harassment had not been established. Thus,

Table 1. What Is Sexual Harassment?

	Males	Females
Is sexual harassment		
Complimentary comments	21.9%	33.5%
Insulting comments	70.3	85.5
Complimentary looks, gestures	18.9	28.9
Insulting looks, gestures	61.6	80.3
Nonsexual touching	6.6	7.3
Sexual touching	58.6	84.3
Expected socializing	91.1	95.8
Expected sexual activity	94.5	98.0

there were no legal or psychological limits to the definition of sexual harassment. Furthermore, I was interested not in sexual harassment alone but in the range of social-sexual interaction between the sexes at work.

The particular categories of behavior studied were developed from two sources. One was our interest in sampling a spectrum of social-sexual behaviors that might be considered sexual harassment. (See Gutek and others, 1980, for details on the rationale for selecting categories.) The second source was the responses obtained in two pilot studies, which led to the addition of two more categories. A total of eight categories of social-sexual behavior were studied: sexual comments meant to be complimentary, sexual comments meant to be insulting, looks and gestures meant to be complimentary, looks and gestures meant to be insulting, nonsexual touching, sexual touching, socializing or dating as a requirement of the job, and sex as a requirement of the job.

Defining Sexual Harassment

We need a definition of sexual harassment before we can tell how common it is. Table 1 shows the percentage of men and women in the survey who thought that a particular kind of behavior is sexual harassment. Over 90 percent of both sexes said they thought that either socializing (or dating) or sexual activity as a job requirement is sexual harassment. In addition, over half of both sexes thought that sexual touching (however they defined it), insulting sexual comments, and sexual gestures meant to be insulting are sexual harassment. Less than 10 percent of both sexes thought nonsexual touching is sexual harassment.

Overall, there is hardly overwhelming consensus among these working people about what constitutes sexual harassment—not surprising when policy makers, lawyers, and personnel officers have the same problem agreeing on a definition. One result that does stand out clearly in Table 1 is the tendency for women to be more likely than men to label each of the categories sexual harassment. Sexual touching shows the biggest gender gap, with 84 percent of the women but only 59 percent of the men considering it sexual harassment.

Overview of Findings

Before we look at the scope and magnitude of sexual harassment in depth, let us consider a brief overview of the findings first.

Trying to measure the frequency of sexual harassment is complicated by the lack of an accepted definition, so I measured it in several ways. From the various analyses that follow, I conclude that sexual harassment is common at work: Up to half of all women experience it at some time in their working lives. Harassment is not as common, however, as other forms of sex at work that are less clearly negative and that are reported by the vast majority of working people.

To my surprise, men reported that they were frequent targets of various kinds of overtures from women. Further analysis showed that few of these incidents appear to be harassment. What men report is numerous sexual overtures from women, which men see as mutually entered and reciprocal. Women, on the other hand, report few mutually enjoyable sexual interchanges. They are more often recipients, frequently unexpected recipients, of both harmless sexual overtures and more serious sexual harassment. Women are the ones who report detrimental consequences of these sexual overtures, including quitting a job and getting fired.

For example, in response to a question about sexual touching, men tend to describe one kind of incident, usually flirtatious behavior by a woman, whereas women tend to describe less complimentary and less flattering overtures that may have ramifications for their job or career.

The Experience of Sexual Harassment

To present the broadest possible view of sexual harassment, I measured it three different ways. First, I assumed all the behaviors listed in Table 1 have the potential of being considered sexual harassment and then could treat everyone who reports any of them as a victim of sexual harassment. This very generous definition undoubtedly overstates the amount of sexual harassment. A second way of defining harassment was to label as sexually harassed those people who experience a behavior and consider that class of behavior to be sexual harassment. Yet a third way of assessing the magnitude of sexual harassment was to have an outside rater determine whether each experience was sexual harassment, on the assumption that a person can be harassed and not know it.

A person might not know she was harassed, if, for example, other people are treated the same way, or if the harasser was unusual in some way. To cite one example, Farley (1978) reported that a woman who worked as a janitor said she was never harassed but was expected to sleep with the foreman if she wanted easy work. Since all the women janitors were subjected to the same treatment, the woman did not consider it harassment but rather a part of the job. To cite another example, one of the women in our survey said it was not harassment when a coworker touched her breasts because he was gay. Based on a reading of laws, regulations, policies, and psychology, a rater would consider both of these incidents harassment.

A rater can also find examples of people who report they are harassed but are not harassed by most standards. During this study, I was a guest on a radio talk show in Washington, D.C. Because the host was intrigued with the idea of men being sexually harassed, he invited sexually harassed men to call in with their stories. Several men's stories were rejected rather quickly until he came to a man who said he was an auto mechanic and a

Table 2. Experiences of Social-Sexual Behaviors.

	Males (N = 405)	Females (N = 827)
Ever experienced on current job		
Complimentary comments	46.0%	50.1%
Insulting comments	12.6	12.2
Complimentary looks, gestures	47.3	51.6
Insulting looks, gestures	12.3	9.1
Nonsexual touching	73.5	68.9
Sexual touching	20.9	15.3
Expected socializing	2.7	2.8
Expected sexual activity	1.0	1.8
Ever experienced on any job		
Complimentary comments	60.7%	68.1%
Insulting comments	19.3	23.3
Complimentary looks, gestures	56.3	66.6
Insulting looks, gestures	19.3	20.3
Nonsexual touching	78.0	74.4
Sexual touching	33.3	33.1
Expected socializing	8.4	12.0
Expected sexual activity	3.5	7.7
Ever experienced and labeled it sexual harassment		
Complimentary comments	10.4%	18.9%
Insulting comments	12.1	19.8
Complimentary looks, gestures	8.1	16.2
Insulting looks, gestures	9.6	15.4
Nonsexual touching	3.5	3.6
Sexual touching	12.3	24.2
Expected socializing	7.4	10.9
Expected sexual activity	3.2	7.6
Have you ever experienced sexual harassment?	37.3%	53.1%

"blonde model with a red sports car" offered to pay in sex rather than money. The radio host asked the man if he was fired or otherwise suffered negative consequences at work for not accepting the woman's offer. When the man said, "Of course not, my boss backed me up 100 percent," the radio host decided that the mechanic had not been harassed. My independent rater would have agreed with him.

Table 2 reports the experiences of men and women with sex at work, and Table 3 reports the rater's decisions. Three sets of figures are shown in Table 2.

Table 3. Sexual Harassment Rating of Open-Ended Responses
by Respondent's Sex.

	Males (N = 122)	Females (N = 281)
Definitely sexual harassment	13.9%	39.1%
Probably sexual harassment	13.9	20.3
Uncertain	32.8	24.6
Probably not sexual harassment	19.7	10.0
Definitely not sexual harassment	19.7	6.0
	100.0%	100.0%

Surprisingly, men report as many sexual overtures as women; in fact, they report significantly more sexual touching than women. This reflects the finding that men are more likely than women to call a touch sexual if the person doing the touching is of the other sex. On the basis of other research (Gutek, Morasch, and Cohen, 1983), I conclude that, in some cases, if a woman touches a man—for example, on the shoulder or the arm—he might consider it sexual, but if a man touched him the same way, he would not consider it sexual. When a man labels a touch sexual, he does not necessarily mean it is inappropriate work behavior; women more often do (Gutek, Morasch, and Cohen, 1983).

Not surprisingly, few people reported that dating or sexual activity is a requirement of their current job. When people are presented with such an ultimatum, they tend to leave the situation by various means: transferring, quitting, or getting fired. Also, perhaps not surprisingly, people were much more likely to report that they are targets of sexual overtures intended to be complimentary than sexual insults.

See the middle of Table 2 for the percentage of men and women who reported each behavior occurring at least once in their entire working lives. The incidence of dating and sexual activity as a job requirement is substantially higher here than as reported for the current job, nearly four times higher. About twice as many women report sexual touching than reported it on their current job.

The final item in Table 2—"Have you ever experienced sexual harassment?"—is the sum of individual experiences, eliminating multiple experiences. Thus, 37.3 percent of the men and

53.1 percent of the women reported experiencing at least one of the social-sexual behaviors that they consider sexual harassment during their working lives. This does not necessarily mean that their own experience is sexual harassment. Rather it means that they experienced something they would generally label sexual harassment.

The third set of figures in Table 2 shows that women were more likely—significantly more likely in all cases except nonsexual touching and expected socializing— than men to experience sexual behavior that they consider sexual harassment. Sexual touching is an interesting case because most of the men who report sexual touching (in the first two sets of figures in Table 2) do not consider it sexual harassment, but most of the women who report sexual touching do consider it harassment. Most of the sexual overtures that were meant to be complimentary were not considered sexual harassment by both sexes, whereas most of the overtures that were meant to be insulting were considered harassment.

Finally, Table 2 clearly shows that the less serious forms of sex at work are much more common than the more serious forms. Most workers have not been faced with an ultimatum like "put out or get out." On the other hand, over half the surveyed women and some men have been sexually harassed sometime during their working lives.

To understand better the kinds of experiences workers had when they reported, for example, that they were sexually touched, the interviewers asked them to talk about the experience. These open-ended responses were obtained for all people who said they were touched sexually on the present or previous job or were asked to date or engage in sexual activity on the present or previous job. These behaviors are generally considered more serious sexual harassment and were the basis for the third measurement of the extent of sexual harassment.

All of the open-ended responses were rated on a variety of dimensions by independent raters. One rater who had first compiled and analyzed various definitions of sexual harassment rated each answer according to how sexually harassing it is. Some of the answers were short or uninformative—"I don't know" or "It's something I don't think about." Such answers (about three dozen for women and two dozen for men) were eliminated from the list of comments to be rated, leaving the comments of 122 men and 281 women.

Table 3 shows the distribution of men and women across the five-point scale showing the judge's ratings of sexual harassment. In general, women's comments were more likely to be rated as sexual harassment than men's comment's were. These figures show that at least 170 women (21 percent of the women surveyed) and 36 men (9 percent of the men surveyed) have been sexually harassed sometime in their working lives. This extremely conservative estimate of sexual harassment no doubt underestimates its occurrence since it only includes people who gave fairly extensive comments about a limited set of behaviors.

This rather involved attempt to measure harassment suggests the following conservative estimate of the frequency of sexual harassment: Between 21 percent and 53 percent of the women and between 9 percent and 37 percent of the men have been sexually harassed by the opposite sex at least once during their working lives. Because the study involved a representative sample of working men and women in Los Angeles County, these figures probably reflect the experiences of the Los Angeles County work force.

What Did Workers Experience? Besides the rater who decided whether or not an experience was sexual harassment, four other raters evaluated people's descriptions of their experiences to understand better exactly what people experienced, which characteristics of an experience made that experience harassment, and how men's and women's experiences differed. The four raters evaluated each of the worker's statements on fourteen different dimensions. Some highlights of this analysis follow.

Men's descriptions of their experiences of being sexually touched or required to date or have sex with a woman at work showed several characteristics generally absent from women's descriptions. For example, men were more likely than women to stress the relationship between themselves and the female initiator. One man said: "The woman was attracted to me, and she wanted to get to know me, I guess. I think she wanted to. . . . We ended up dating; it led to a relationship. And, as a matter of fact, we were dating." Men's descriptions also tended to mention some positive outcomes of the interchange, whereas none of the women's comments did. One man said: "There was a natural attraction between the two of us. We ended up seeing each other quite a lot."

Not surprisingly, men's comments also tended to be concerned with mutuality—mutual physical attraction or liking—whereas none of the women's experiences was rated high on this dimension. One man's comments: "Probably because we were attracted to each other. It was a personal attraction rather than what could be gained professionally. There was no consideration on both parts of job gain or job advancement."

The descriptions of women's experiences of sexual touching, dating, and sexual activity as part of the job showed several characteristics absent from men's descriptions. For example, although none of the men's comments emphasized a negative outcome, several women did. One woman said: "Probably because he was a jerk. It was his business and he probably thought it was his right to ask me to have sexual relations with him. I was very young at the time and it was my first job. I quit after three weeks."

Certain conditions such as office parties and business trips may facilitate both intimacy and harassment between the sexes. The same set of conditions—an office party, for example—could create an opportunity to strike up a sexual friendship or to get drunk and harass coworkers. None of the men mentioned such a negative condition or situation whereas several of the women did; one woman presumed that the overture was partly an outcome of the man's divorce. "Probably because he was divorced and I'm pretty good looking. He was antsy. Like, if it wasn't me, he would approach someone else. [It was the] boss I had. [It] wasn't that I would have lost my job, but there were certain advantages in the office had I gone out with him."

Several times women attributed the man's behavior to his drunkenness, as one stewardess noted, "He just expected it of us. He was drunk. Guess he just figured the stereotype: All stewardesses are prostitutes. You expect it. Mostly businessmen who fly a lot consider us sex objects." Another woman observed:

> He drank a lot. When he was cold sober, he
> didn't act that way. When he drank, which was often,
> he'd try to put his arms around you and kiss you.
> I'd just take my purse and bash him with it. He
> didn't remember what he had done while he was
> drunk. When he was sober, he'd apologize for what-
> ever he had done.

Women's comments differed from men's in yet another
way. Women frequently mentioned other recipients or victims,
whereas men did not. For example: "He was behind me. I was
the only one. It was just his personality. I never led the man on.
You didn't have to. He was like an octopus. I never liked the man.
And all the other women in the plant had a problem with him
also. He'd try to catch different women by themselves when no
one else was looking." And: "Testing to see what would happen.
I made it clear it better not happen again. He thought he was 'a
killer.' Tried it on all the women."

On other dimensions assessed by the four raters, men's and
women's comments were similar. For example, women and men
were equally likely to emphasize their own characteristics and to
stereotype the other sex. The following are two comments, by a
man and a woman, in which they focus on themselves:

> There was a physical attractiveness. I was
> much younger and much more promiscuous, just out
> of high school. It led to other things. Bigger and
> better. Started off by kidding each other. Led up to
> going out to "your place or mine?"

> The man is a breast man. I have beautiful
> breasts and he just reached out. It was a man's nor-
> mal reaction to an attractive woman. We spent hours
> together; the familiarity invites this kind of thing.

In their descriptions of their own experiences, some people
relied on stereotypes: "That's the way men [or women] are." Men
and women were both likely to make such remarks, women somewhat more so than men. In one man's view of women, "They let
you know they are available. They look forward to free meals. I
haven't been anywhere where women aren't looking for men."

One woman summed up her view: "Some men like to make passes at women. They think a waitress is fair game."

In summary, women stressed (1) the possibilities of a negative outcome from the interchange, (2) the conditions leading up to the overture, and (3) the man's attention to other victims or targets. Men stressed (1) the relationship between the initiator and target, (2) the mutuality in the incident, and (3) the positive outcomes of the incident, which were exclusively personal rather than work related.

Not surprisingly, for both sexes the experience was less likely to be considered sexual harassment by the rater when mutuality or the relationship between the two parties was stressed in the comments. The experience was more likely to be labeled sexual harassment when conditions affecting the incident or some characteristics of the initiator were stressed. In general, these relationships were stronger for women than for men. Other aspects of the experience were rated differently when they were reported by a man versus a woman. For example, when women discussed the initiator in any way, the incident was frequently judged sexual harassment but this was not true for men. On the other hand, when men discussed themselves in their comments, the incident was less frequently judged to be sexual harassment.

These findings show that men's and women's comments about their own experiences of sex at work are different in predictable ways. Are they sufficiently different that one could guess whether a man or a woman made any specific comment? I tried to do just that. The file of comments was rewritten, obliterating all reference to the gender of the commenter. For example, "She was drunk and feeling loose. We handled her like any other drunk" became: "S/HE was drunk and feeling loose. We handled HIM/HER like any other drunk."

Words that were changed for the judges were capitalized. Where it was difficult to substitute a sex-neutral term, the word was "x'd" out. "Waitress" was removed here "I was a xxxxx in a diner. In order to get my paycheck, S/HE wanted a kiss. The other xxxx told me to put up with HIM/HER. I quit after three weeks. I had to take HIM/HER to small claims court to get my check. They fined HIM/HER $1,200. S/HE was really a jerk."

Four judges then guessed whether the comment was made by a man or a woman. Only 6.5 percent of the men's comments were judged as probably or definitely made by women, and only 12.5 percent of the women's comments were judged as probably or definitely said by men. The relationship between actual sex of a person and guessed sex was high. These results add evidence to the contention that men and women are reporting very different kinds of sexual touching, required dating, and required sex on the job, although I admit that our attempts to obliterate all reference to gender were not successful. Many clues remain even after substituting gender neutral words. For example, men rarely describe women as "jerks," and women rarely describe men as "loose." The situations also provide clues. For example, it is difficult to picture a woman demanding a kiss from a man before she gives him his paycheck.

What can we conclude from this analysis of people's experiences? First, sexual harassment is common, and women are the most likely victims. Harassment may take the form of comments, gestures, leering, and touching as well as dating or sex as a requirement of the job. Men report almost as many overtures from women under some circumstances, but men are more likely to view such encounters positively, to see them as fun and mutually entered. A high proportion of the more serious incidents reported by men are sexual touching, but by their own reports, many do not view sexual touching as sexual harassment. Furthermore, most of the sexual touching they describe tends not to be rated as harassment by outside raters. Although women report some mutually entered experiences, they report more experiences that they find uncomfortable and unpleasant. Just how uncomfortable some of these encounters are can be understood in part by finding the lengths to which people will go to avoid them.

Consequences of Sexual Harassment. The majority of people in the survey did not think sexual harassment was a problem at their current workplaces. Only 3 percent of the women and 1 percent of the men said it was a major problem; 20 percent of the women and 21 percent of the men called it a minor problem.

Despite these low reports of problems, a substantial number of women have taken rather drastic measures to avoid, or try to

Table 4. Percentages of Respondents Experiencing Negative Consequences of Sexual Harassment.

	Women	Men
Ever quit job because sexually harassed?	9.1%	1.0%
Ever transfer because sexually harassed?	5.1	0.2
Ever talk to a coworker about sexual harassment?	22.5	5.5
Ever quit trying for a job because you were sexually harassed?	9.6	1.2
Ever lose a job because you refused sex?	6.9	2.2

deal with, sexual harassment. Table 4 shows that about 9 percent of the women have quit a job sometime because they refused to grant sexual favors. Altogether, 31 percent of women reported one or more of the consequences shown in Table 4.

The corresponding and much lower figures for men are consistent with men's own reports of their experiences with sex at work. Men do not feel sexually harassed, and their experiences—although common by their reports—do not lead to a transfer or loss of a job. The sexual experiences of men at work appear to have no job-related consequences for them, at least not negative ones.

Victims of Sexual Harassment

In her book about cases of sexual harassment, Farley (1978) carefully cited instances of sexual harassment among many groups of working women: young and old, rich and poor, professional and unskilled. She contended that sexual harassment was endemic to the workplace and did not happen only to a select group of women. The Los Angeles County survey results generally corroborate her belief. Sexual harassment is not just a problem for one or two employed groups. It is likely to happen to almost any female worker. A brief summary follows of the personal characteristics of men and women victims of harassment: their age, marital status, presence or absence of children, education, occupation, family income, and ethnicity. The key result is that none of these characteristics is as important as sex. Women are more likely to be harassed than men, so I begin by examining the personal characteristics of women that affect their experience of sex at work.

Female Victims. Female victims tend to be younger than the general female working population. About 60 percent of the women who have quit a job because of sexual harassment are thirty-five or under. Of the women who reported experiencing sexual harassment on the current job, 57 percent are thirty-five or under. Although women over thirty-five are not immune to sexual harassment, younger women who are perhaps less experienced with work and harassment, and perhaps more desirable targets for men, are more often victims.

Marital status is strongly related to sexual harassment. Working women who are married or widowed are less likely to be harassed than working women who are divorced, separated, or never married. Although never-married women make up 22 percent of the sample, 31 percent of the women who quit a job because of sexual harassment have never been married. And whereas divorced and separated women make up 20 percent of the sample, they represent 27 percent of the victims of sexual harassment, according to the independent rater's assessment of harassment.

Whether a woman has children or not was not specifically related to harassment. Thirty-eight percent of the women in the study have children, and 36 percent of those who reported sexual harassment have children.

Women who are well educated are generally as likely to be sexually harassed as women who are less well educated. If anything, victims of harassment are even more likely to have advanced education. Perhaps women without advanced education generally tolerate undesirable working conditions and put up with sexual harassment as part of the job. Several waitresses in the study, for example, said that waitresses have to expect unwelcome sexual advances in their work, so some of them may not report harassment.

Women with advanced degrees are likely to be occupationally vulnerable if not particularly financially vulnerable. That is, their careers may be more dependent on a particular job at a particular time than a less-educated person who may leave one unskilled job—as waitress, for example—for another comparable job with relative ease. The ambitious woman in advertising, however, may really want a job with one of several prestigious firms. The same is true for the aspiring lawyer, researcher, manager, or college professor. The career-minded lawyer is not likely to leave a prestigious law firm unless she has an equally good job elsewhere. Similarly, an assistant professor at a highly regarded university is not likely to say "I don't have to put up with that; I'll quit," whereas the waitress at a run-of-the-mill restaurant may take just such an approach. Thus, the woman with advanced degrees may be a particularly vulnerable target because her specific job is valuable to her. In addition, she probably has higher expectations for being treated in a professional manner so she may be more inclined to label sexual overtures harassment than the person who expects sexual overtures as part of the job.

Women of all occupations are about equally likely to be sexually harassed, although women managers are slightly more likely than other women to be harassed. Managers constituted 8 percent of the sample of women, but 13 percent of the people harassed were managers. Among the well-educated women, managers may be particularly vulnerable since they are viewed as especially ambitious (and perhaps willing to "do anything" to advance).

Women at all income levels may be sexually harassed. Sexual harassment is not something that happens just to poor women. Family income is a generally reasonable measure of financial vulnerability. As the results on education suggest, women may be financially or occupationally vulnerable, and sexual harassment occurs to both groups.

The survey results suggest that minority women are not particularly more vulnerable to sexual harassment than Caucasian women. In fact, Caucasian women report somewhat higher rates of sexual harassment and are more likely to quit a job because of sexual harassment. A variety of factors may contribute to these findings; minority women may report fewer of their experiences and Caucasian women may represent the cultural standard of attractiveness.

In sum, an attempt to develop a demographic profile of

the sexually harassed woman has not been particularly fruitful. The one characteristic clearly related to sexual harassment is marital status. Being married or widowed leads to fewer experiences of harassment relative to women who are single, divorced, separated, or living with a man. Perhaps women who are married or widowed are viewed as being under a man's protection that other men honor. Other women are then "fair game." Younger women are also more likely than older women to report being sexually harassed, a result that is consistent with the protection hypothesis.

Except for marital status, other demographic characteristics—education, income, and occupation—that one might expect to be important were not. A high-status job does not prevent women from being sexually harassed.

Male Victims. A man's age is not consistently related to his being sexually harassed. According to men's self-reports, the average victim is slightly younger than the average worker. According to the independent rater, the average male victim is slightly older than the average male worker. This discrepancy arises because the reports of young men were hardly ever judged by the rater to be sexual harassment. Young men were particularly likely to report and describe sex but not sexual harassment.

Married men are somewhat less likely to report experiences of sexual harassment than are unmarried men. Being married apparently inhibits colleagues from making overtures. Married men, like married women, are "already taken." The two groups of men who received a disproportionate share of overtures are divorced men and men living with a woman. These results parallel the findings for women workers. What is different for the two sexes is that never-married men were not more likely to be sexually harassed whereas never-married women were more likely to be harassed.

Men who report instances of sexual harassment on the job were just as likely to have children as men who were not sexually harassed. Education also was not related to being sexually harassed among men, just as it was not related to sexual harassment among women.

In general, men in different occupational categories did not report instances of sexual harassment more often, except for men in managerial positions and service work. For example, although 16 percent of the men said they were managers, of those reporting sexual harassment, 19 percent were managers; of those judged to have experienced sexual harassment by the independent rater, 25 percent were managers.

As with education and occupation, family income was not related to being sexually harassed. Just as with women, men with different incomes are equally likely to be harassed.

Ethnicity is not significantly related to sexual harassment among men. Although the sample sizes are too small to produce reliable findings, the results suggest that minority men have a slightly higher probability of being harassed than white men.

In summary, as in the case of women, marital status was the only demographic characteristic strongly related to experiencing sexual harassment. Women and men who do not belong to someone else are apparently perceived as fair game and, perhaps, more approachable than other workers. Divorced and separated men and those living with a woman seem to be targets for women's overtures.

Summary

Sex at work is not a rare phenomenon; neither is sexual harassment. Between one quarter and one half of all women have been sexually harassed sometime during their working lives. Women who are single, separated, or divorced are more likely to be sexually harassed; being young exacerbates the problem. Over 20 percent of women have quit a job, been transferred, been fired, or quit applying for a job because of sexual harassment. This represents a fairly substantial loss for organizations, directly through the loss of these employees and indirectly through lowered morale, as well as lowered commitment to the job where they were harassed and possibly to future jobs.

Although sexual harassment is widespread, it is not always easily distinguished from mutually entered social-sexual exchanges because one of the parties may be intentionally hiding his or her feelings. This stance is more often taken by the woman. Perhaps she does not want to hurt the man or is afraid of negative repercussions if she were open about her feelings. This fear of repercussions is understandable since women are more likely than men to suffer adverse consequences of such encounters.

In other circumstances, a woman may feign sexual interest (although she has none) because she feels she will be promoted or given special favors or because she feels such an attitude is the only way to catch an influential man's attention. In his study of third-party reports of office romances, Quinn (1977) found that one common pattern of office romance involved a woman who was interested in an instrumental relationship and a man who was interested in a "fling" or affair. Given the dismal picture of women's occupational attainment in general, dispensing sexual favors clearly does not open the doors to the executive suite, although it may lead to little favors: a new typewriter, a trip to San Francisco, a busier or lighter set of tables to wait on. However, sex may work as well (or as poorly) as anything else as a way to be noticed. A woman who is frustrated by her attempts to have her work noticed or to have an opportunity to take on new responsibilities may attempt to use sexual flattery or flirtatious behavior as a way to gain some attention. Once she has been noticed, she may have real difficulty trying to redirect the man's attention from her sexuality to her work (see Kanter, 1977a).

Some of the experiences reported may involve not different motives or intentions but merely different perceptions. Because men are used to being sexual initiators, some may view anything short of physical resistance as consent by women. There may be substantial disagreement about the interpretation of any particular encounter, given that men reported significantly more mutually entered interchanges than did women. Whereas the man may see the event as mutual, the woman may describe it quite differently. More than one woman in the survey mentioned a man who thought he was a "lady killer" or "thought he could have every woman in the office." But the women in the survey and their coworkers did not share this man's perceptions of himself.

Obtaining two people's views of the same incident was not possible with the survey data, but a simulation study my students and I did permitted men and women to evaluate an identical hypothetical encounter (Gutek, Morasch, and Cohen, 1983). In that study, men were significantly more likely than women to view the social-sexual encounter as sexual and were significantly more likely than women to view it as appropriate behavior. Apparently, some men do not view sexual exchanges as incompatible with appropriate work behavior, perhaps because they rarely experience negative repercussions themselves.

In general, women and men seem to have differing perceptions about what is appropriate behavior at work, they may have different intentions and motives when they make sexual advances, and they are differentially affected by sex at work. Women are more likely to be sexually harassed (by an independent rater's evaluation of their comments) and to feel sexually harassed. Women are the ones who suffer job-related consequences of harassment, too. They are more likely than men to quit or otherwise lose jobs because of unwanted sexual advances.

Although a lot of women and some men are sexually harassed, even more report experiences that they do not consider harassment. Most of the sex at work is not defined as a problem by the individuals involved or by their organizations. About 80 percent of the workers in the survey reported one or more social-sexual experiences that they would not consider harassment. People who are intimate with a work colleague or who are flattered by an actual or imagined advance may wonder about the fuss over sexual harassment. They may not be able to distinguish between their own encouragement of sexual overtures and another person's anguish over being harassed. The people (all men) in the survey who volunteered that they would "love to be harassed" fall into this group. The high incidence of sex at work that represents caring, intimacy, flattery, and plain physical attraction no doubt contributes to the difficulty in defining sexual harassment.

In addition, victims of sexual harassment are not easily distinguished from other workers. Attempts to profile victims of sexual harassment were not especially fruitful. Marital status is the characteristic most strongly related to being sexually harassed for both sexes.

The next chapter focuses on the harassers, the relationship between the harasser and victim, and the reactions of victims that affect them and their organization.

FOUR

Characteristics of Harassers and Reactions of Victims

This chapter examines the harassers and their victims. In looking at victims' responses to the harassment, including their great reluctance to formally complain about it, the chapter explains why women are reluctant to make complaints. One important outcome of this examination is a picture of responses of sexual harassment victims, a picture quite different from the one organizations see as defendants of lawsuits.

Until now, the only information we had on harassers came from stories, anecdotes, and gossip about colleagues, bosses, and acquaintances who sexually exploit others at work, plus a few sensational cases that received extensive media coverage, usually because they involved a well-known person. Because it is difficult to get people to talk about their own experiences as harassers at work, most reports about initiators are from recipients. Of course, recipients are likely to have limited information about the harasser, and some of that information may be biased by that person's experiences, presumably unpleasant, with the initiator.

Who Makes Sexual Advances?

According to the women and men in the survey, the men who make advances toward women are very different from the women who make advances toward men. The "average" man who

Table 1. Profile of Initiators.

How Long Associated with Initiator?

	Less than 1 day	Less than 2 months	2–6 months	Over 6 months	Total (N)
Female Recipients	5.8	20.0	24.2	50.0	100% (310)
Male Recipients	5.6	23.8	25.2	45.5	100% (143)

Initiator Behaves This Way Toward Others

	Yes	No	Total (N)
Female Recipients	71.0	29.0	100% (259)
Male Recipients	52.3	47.7	100% (109)

Initiator Is a Supervisor

	Yes	No	Total (N)
Female Recipients	44.8	56.3	100% (306)
Male Recipients	5.5	94.5	100% (139)

Initiator Age

	Under 30	30–39	40–49	Over 50	Total (N)
Female Recipients	19.0	31.8	26.0	23.1	100% (311)
Male Recipients	56.6	34.4	9.0	0.0	100% (145)

Initiator Married

	Yes	No	Total (N)
Female Recipients	65.4	34.6	100% (288)
Male Recipients	28.4	71.6	100% (131)

Attractiveness of Initiator

	Above average	Not above average	Total (N)
Female Recipients	41.8	58.2	100% (306)
Male Recipients	71.6	28.4	100% (141)

propositions or harasses a woman is much like the "average" working man on the dimensions measured in the survey. In contrast to men, the "average" woman who makes advances is not at all typical of the "average" working woman.

Table 1 shows the characteristics of male and female initiators of sexual touching and dating or sexual activity as a requirement of the job, whether or not the particular experiences were considered sexual harassment by the recipients or by an independent rater. Three aspects of the relationship between the initiator and recipient were measured, and three characteristics of the initiator—age, marital status, and physical attractiveness—were assessed.

Working men and women differ in describing the men and women who make advances, as Table 1 indicates. Both sexes reported that the two people were most likely to have been associated for at least six months. About 6 percent of men and women reported an incident on the same day they met the initiator. Sexual incidents involving new customers, clients, or salespeople are only a small percentage of sexual incidents.

Women and men reported large differences in the other five areas shown in Table 1. Consistent with some findings reported in the previous chapter, women were more likely than men to say that the initiator behaved the same way toward others at work. Women were also much more likely than men to say that the initiator was a supervisor. However, fewer than half of the male initiators were women's supervisors, suggesting that the majority of sexual advances at work are directed toward peers, not subordinates.

With respect to personal characteristics of initiators, men are more likely than women to describe initiators as young, unmarried, and attractive. According to men, fewer than 10 percent of female initiators are over forty and half are under thirty. Over 70 percent of female initiators are unmarried and above average in physical attractiveness. Male initiators are older (almost half are forty or over), predominantly married, and less attractive.

The male initiators resemble the average working men in the survey. Of the men in the sample, 53 percent are thirty-six or over and 68 percent of them are married. By comparison, 49 percent of the initiators are forty or over and 65 percent are married. On the other hand, female initiators are younger and less likely to be married than the average working woman; 21 percent of the surveyed women are under twenty-five, and another 29 percent are between twenty-six and thirty-five. By comparison,

57 percent of the initiators are under thirty, and 91 percent are under forty. Half the working women in the sample are married, but only 28 percent of the female initiators are married.

In summary, the women in the study describe an average male initiator who is much like the average male worker with the exception that the initiator tends to behave the same way toward other women workers. The male harassers are similar to other working men, at least on the set of characteristics measured in this study.

On the other hand, men describe a female initiator who is not at all like the average female worker. The average woman who makes advances is young, attractive, not married, and not a supervisor. It seems unlikely that such a female employee is in an organizational position to harass anyone. But much of the sex described by men was not viewed as sexual harassment either by them or by an independent rater (see Chapter Three). So it is possible that the female initiators are substantially different from the female harassers (since most of what these women initiated was not considered harassment).

To see if the characteristics of harassers differ from initiators and to determine whether the descriptions of male and female harassers are more alike than those of male and female initiators, the analyses shown in Table 1 were rerun twice. One analysis used only those respondents who called their own experiences sexual harassment (that is, they labeled the category of behavior as sexual harassment). The second analysis used only the experiences that the independent rater called sexual harassment.

The results of these two analyses showed that, in general, "harassers" were not very different from "initiators," and the differences in the way men and women described initiators persisted in their descriptions of harassers. Compared to initiators, harassers generally were a little older, a little more likely to be married and be supervisors, slightly less attractive, a little more likely to behave the same toward others, and somewhat less likely to have a long association with the recipient. All of the discrepancies between harassers and initiators are in the direction one would expect. However, the male harassers were still significantly different from the female harassers, although these analyses were based on smaller subsamples. (For example, the experiences of only 34 men and 165 women were judged by the rater as probably or definitely sexual harassment.)

There were some small differences in the way workers defined harassers as compared to initiators. For example, whereas 72 percent of female initiators were rated above average in attractiveness, 64 percent of female harassers (using the independent rating to measure harassment) were above average in attractiveness. Whereas 45 percent of male initiators were supervisors, 50 percent of male harassers were supervisors. Thus, more of the overtures made by supervisors, in comparison to nonsupervisors, were considered harassment by the independent rater.

In general, the other descriptions of initiators and harassers (using both criteria of harassment) were within a few percentage points of each other, although the harasser sample was one third the size of the initiator sample for men and one half the initiator sample for women. Thus, even the men's incidents labeled sexual harassment tended to involve a young, attractive, nonsupervisory, unmarried woman. These results are not easy to explain. One point to keep in mind is that only 8.5 percent of the men reported an incident that was either definitely or probably sexual harassment (according to the independent rater). In these cases, it is not an older female supervisor who is the harasser but rather an unmarried, young, attractive coworker, subordinate, or customer, who is unlikely to be in a position to affect the man's work performance or chances for promotion.

A likely description of these incidents is flirtatious or seductive behavior—what one man in the survey called "trying to get in good with the boss." These incidents are not harassment in the way it is usually conceptualized, that is, as having adverse job-related consequences. An attractive, unmarried, young woman may behave seductively because she is sexually or romantically interested in the man, wants to acquire extra privileges at work, is trying to have her work noticed, or wants access to useful, job-relevant information. It is unlikely that she can affect the man's job, although she may constitute an annoyance or an embarrassment to him. While such behavior on the part of a woman may be persuasive or even irresistible to the man, it lacks any organizational authority of the kind possessed by a foreman or manager making sexual demands of a subordinate. If the man does find the situation too bothersome or embarrassing, he probably can transfer the woman or even fire her for nonprofessional conduct, as one man in the survey said he did. The subordinate subject to overtures from a supervisor does not have that option.

Interactions Between Harassers and Their Targets

The most common kind of sexual encounter at work involves a female recipient and a male initiator who behaves the same way toward other women. To examine these relationships in more detail, questions about the type of interaction between the two and responses to the incident were asked in the follow-up survey involving women who were sexually touched or expected to engage in social or sexual activity with a man at work. The 135 women interviewed in the follow-up survey did not differ significantly from the women who could not be contacted on several key variables such as age, kind of social-sexual experience, or feelings of responsibility for the experience (Jensen, 1981).

So far, the analysis of sex at work reported in this chapter and in Chapter Three has proceeded by focusing on a single, specific incident and examining the characteristics of that incident, the target, and the initiator. One question that comes to mind is what leads up to, or elicits, these incidents? After several weeks, months, or years of working together, does one person suddenly grab or proposition another? Such a scenario is not particularly compatible with the sex role spillover perspective. If men respond to women in a way consistent with sex role expectations, one would expect other interactions also to be influenced by sex role expectations, although not all of them would necessarily be sexual harassment or even sexual. A man who responds to a woman at work in a manner consistent with sex role expectations might assume she likes to hear how attractive she is, but might also assume she enjoys playing a nurturing role, for example.

An examination of the kinds of discussions between initiators and their targets supports this view. Men who make advances toward women hardly ever talk about the woman's work performance or her career with her, although only twenty-one women in the survey said that they did not have to interact with the man during their work. For the large majority of these harasser-victim pairs, interacting was necessary to their work, yet the men did not tend to discuss work.

Instead, the man tends to talk about himself, his personal life and problems, and matters of mutual interest unrelated to work (hobbies, sports, and the like). These topics suggest a high degree of self-absorption on the part of the man. He talks about matters that concern him. An even more likely topic of conversation than the man's concerns is the woman's personal appearance and clothing. About one third of the men who made advances commented frequently about the woman's clothing or appearance. Only 19 percent never did so, but 38 percent never commented on her work performance or career.

Some men apparently think it unnecessary to discuss work performance with women who interact with them on the job. It is possible that these men have little interest in their own work, but perhaps they think women are not very interested in or committed to their work, which may seem unimportant. Or perhaps they think women prefer to hear comments about their appearance rather than about their work. Perhaps some men think women at work enjoy hearing about men's interests and problems and are flattered when their advice is sought about personal matters. All of these possibilities view women in accordance with sex role expectations rather than work requirements and thus are consistent with the sex role spillover perspective. These results also show that men who make serious sexual overtures toward women tend to treat women as women rather than as workers. Although from the target woman's point of view, there is a big difference between frequent comments about her personal appearance and a demand for sexual compliance, both are similar from the sex role spillover perspective: They emphasize a woman's femaleness over her role as a worker.

The patterns of discussion between the man and the female recipient are not affected much by the relationship between the two. Men who view their female colleagues and subordinates primarily as women rather than as workers tend to show a consistent style of interaction whether or not they are the woman's supervisor. A supervisor was slightly (but not significantly) more likely than other initiators to discuss things he valued with the female recipient. Supervisors were neither more nor less likely to discuss the woman's physical appearance but were more likely than non-supervisors to discuss her career or job performance.

Men who, according to women's reports, make overtures toward other women are more likely than other initiators to discuss the woman recipient's physical appearance. And discussion about the man's personal interests was more common when the man and woman had to interact in the course of work.

Some male initiators apparently use their positions as supervisors or coworkers to discuss their own personal interests with some women at work. Presumably, these men think their comments and discussions are welcome and may be surprised to find out that the female recipients do not share their viewpoint. In addition, men who frequently comment on women's physical appearance apparently do so to many women. They seem more likely than other men to be labeled the "office wolf" or local "womanizer." While some of these men may be attractive to the women they work with, they may more commonly be described, to use the words of the women in the survey, as "a real jerk," "a gross man," or "a drip with an overinflated ego." In addition, some of the men might be attractive to a woman in another setting, but women resent their overtures at work, their thorough confounding of work roles and sex roles.

Responsibility for Incidents

Both the main survey and the follow-up survey directed a series of questions toward one serious incident of social-sexual behavior and explored why the incident occurred. According to the main survey results, both sexes felt little responsibility for the incident. Men and women who were expected to have sex as a condition of work in some previously held job were asked specifically how responsible they felt for the incident. Overall, 61 percent of the women and 45 percent of the men said they were not at all responsible for the incident. In describing their most serious instance of sexual harassment, men were more likely than women to say they were partially responsible for the incident. In this case, respondents were evaluating their most serious instance of sexual touching, social dating, or sex as a requirement of work. When this broader group of social-sexual behaviors is considered, 51 percent of the men say they were either somewhat or very responsible for what happened, but only 15 percent of the women say they were either somewhat or very responsible for the incident.

Both sexes were more likely to admit some responsibility for the incident if the initiator was physically attractive. This finding can be interpreted two ways: Workers welcome overtures from attractive people, or workers perceive as attractive those people whose attention they encourage. One other finding was significant for women only. Women were less likely to accept responsibility for the incident if the initiating man behaved the same way toward other women than if he behaved that way toward the respondent only. There was no relationship between these two variables for men.

In summary, men were more likely than women to feel that their actions contributed to being approached by the other sex, and both sexes were more likely to admit responsibility for the incident if the initiator was attractive. These findings help to explain the puzzling results reported earlier about female harassers. Men may have encouraged some of the overtures from young women including overtures that were labeled harassment. The findings that both sexes also admit more responsibility when the initiator is attractive and men were more likely to describe their harassers as attractive lend further support to the contention.

The issue of responsibility for the incident was explored in greater depth in the follow-up study of 135 women victims of sexual harassment. Several questions were asked to see how much the recipient blamed herself, the initiator, and the atmosphere at work for the incident. One kind of self-blame is typified by the comment of a harassed woman in the study: "Anything that happens to you is your own fault."

The survey explored four sources of blame: the male harasser, the atmosphere at work, the victim's behavior, and the victim's character. These last two sources involve aspects of self-blame and correspond closely to Janoff-Bulman's (1979) distinction between behavioral self-blame and characterological self-blame.

In assessing blame, 70 percent of the women who were harassed blamed the man who initiated the overture. In contrast, 12 percent agreed strongly agreed that the atmosphere at work was at fault, 10 percent agreed strongly that they were "the sort of person" who had such experiences, and less than 2 percent agreed strongly that their own behavior was to blame. Although self-blame was uncommon, a significant minority of the women exhibited some self-blame; 18 percent agreed at least somewhat that their behavior contributed to their own harassment, and 22 percent agreed at least somewhat that they were the sort of person who had such experiences. These women apparently tend to expect "things like this," unpleasant experiences that seem to happen to them but not to others. (The issue of self-blame is explored in greater detail in Jensen, 1981, and in Jensen and Gutek, 1982.)

Reactions to Sexual Harassment

The survey explored two kinds of reactions to sexual harassment. First, it examined the psychological reactions of the women—their feelings and the effects of the harassment on their work and their relationships with others at work and elsewhere. Second, it explored the extent to which victims of harassment turn to their employers for help, why they do, and why they do not.

Although women overwhelmingly blamed men for harassment, they were generally satisfied with the way the incident was resolved. Fifty-four percent of the women were satisfied with how they handled the harassment, and 79 percent were confident they could handle any future overtures. On the other hand, 16 percent were not satisfied with the way the incident was handled, and a sizable minority reported a variety of negative effects from the incident. Thirty-eight percent of the women said the incident affected their feelings about their jobs and 28 percent said it affected how they relate to other people at work. In general, the harassment had a greater effect on work than it did on the woman's private life, although about 15 percent of the women reported that the incident affected their health or their relationships with other men.

The women in the survey also were asked how they felt right after the incident. The two strongest reactions were disgust and anger: over two fifths of the women said they felt disgust and about one third said they were angry. Fewer women (under 15 percent) reported feeling anxious or hurt, and fewer than 10 percent said they felt very depressed, sad, or guilty. Remember that they were reporting reactions to events that occurred over a year ago. Some initial hurt, for example, may have turned to anger over time. In addition, many of the strong emotions the women felt at the time of the harassment may have been forgotten a year later.

One possible, and appropriate, reaction to sexual harassment is to report it to a supervisor or proper official at work. In 1980, when the survey was done, many large companies already had some policy about sexual harassment. Even without a specific policy, organizations have procedures for accepting and processing a variety of complaints about employment practices. In general, available research reveals that very few women report incidents of harassment to authorities (U.S. Merit Systems Protection Board, 1981; Dunwoody-Miller and Gutek, 1985), and the women in the survey were no different. Only 24 of 135 victims interviewed in the follow-up study reported the incident to someone in authority. Thirty percent of the women who were harassed said that reporting the incident would just hurt them, and another 24 percent said the man involved might be hurt. Thus, a sizable number of harassment victims apparently think that reporting the harassment is just going to lead to trouble. They are concerned not only about themselves but also about the harasser. Although many women are angered or disgusted by the man's behavior, they most often do not want to hurt him in any way. Some people may believe that women who file complaints against men at work are vindictive and spiteful, but the survey responses revealed that many more are compassionate and forgiving.

To understand more about victims' views of their organization's response to harassment, the women who did not make a complaint or otherwise report the sexual harassment they experienced were asked why they did not do so. Sixty percent of the nonreporters thought they would be blamed for the incident if they made a formal complaint. Sixty percent also said they thought nothing would be done and that complaining about the harassment would make work unpleasant for everyone. In addition, 66 percent said they did not report the incident because they thought the man involved could be hurt if the incident was reported. And 31 percent said they were too embarrassed to report the incident.

On the other hand, 32 percent said reporting the incident took too much time and effort, and 82 percent of the women who did not report the incident said that they saw no real need to report it. It may seem curious that although the vast majority of women blamed the male initiator for their sexual harassment, many women felt disgust or anger in response, and a sizable minority of women reported ill effects, the majority did not see any need to report the incident. One may guess that many did not report the harassment because they were concerned about the negative repercussions of reporting it or perhaps the sheer waste of their time if the complaint would just languish on someone's desk. In general, the women who did not report the incident were more likely than others to blame themselves for the harassment, especially if they thought their behavior brought about the incident. Women who blamed themselves were also somewhat more likely to say they did not want to hurt the harasser (see also Jensen, 1981).

This combination of findings suggests that women may feel more responsibility than they are willing to admit, or, perhaps, they feel they have no right to expect anything different, although they did not cause the event. Little in these findings shows that women feel they will receive support within their organizations if they object to such behavior. The overall picture is one of resignation to such incidents.

Note also that these reports are retrospective; the women are recalling incidents that occurred over a year prior to the interview. They most likely had come to some resolution about the experience. Whether or not they had taken some action, they probably had rationalized or justified their behavior.

While the majority of women do not blame themselves for the experience, they still feel it is their responsibility to handle the problem themselves, and they may feel they have failed to properly control the situation. This result is consistent with a study of managers (Collins and Blodgett, 1981) indicating that managers feel that women should be able to deal with advances and propositions. It is part of the job.

Summary

The findings in this chapter add evidence to the assertion that sexual harassment of men is rare. Chapter Three showed that very few men have ever quit a job or been fired because of sexual harassment. This chapter showed that some men said they were at least partially responsible for the incidents and suggests they might have encouraged overtures from young, attractive, unmarried female coworkers or subordinates. It is not clear whether all the harassment reported by men can be attributed to their own complicity, but it is increasingly clear that men are rarely harassed the way women are. The next chapter, in which women and men speak for themselves about their own experiences and concerns about sex at work, adds further corroboration. In contrast to the experiences of men, harassment experienced by women more readily conforms to the general definition of sexual harassment.

On the basis of the social characteristics measured in this study, the average male harasser was virtually indistinguishable from other working men with respect to age, marital status, and physical attractiveness. But most harassers approach more than one woman, and women tend to be aware that they are not the only victim. Engaging in social talk and discussion of women's appearance, they respond to their female colleagues and subordinates as potential sexual partners rather than as coworkers, and they respond to women on the basis of sex role expectations not work role requirements.

Women are angered and disgusted by this attention. Most

of them place all of the blame on the man, but feel it is their own responsibility to handle the matter and want to do so without hurting the man. When the situation gets out of hand, they may quit, ask for a transfer, or be asked to leave, but they rarely report the incident to authorities. Women who blame themselves for the incident are even more concerned than others about hurting the man and are less likely than other women to report the incident.

For many women, leaving the job may seem like less effort than filing a complaint. To file a complaint, they must first find the appropriate department or agency. This in itself is work when one lacks confidence that anything will come from the formal complaint. If anything does happen, they fear that they will be the one who suffers or that the man's career will be jeopardized. Some alternative that stops the harassment without ruining careers and that spares the organization a lengthy, emotionally draining, and costly investigation seems attractive. In many cases, the woman simply decides that leaving the job is the least painful alternative for her, even though her own career will suffer. (She may perceive that if she makes a formal complaint, her career will suffer at least as much.) In such a case, her replacement may be subject to the same harassment. One of the biggest losers here is the organization.

Implications for Management

Most of the women who were harassed up to the time of the study, the summer of 1980, did not report the harassment to anyone in their organization for a variety of reasons. What managers should appreciate is that for every woman who complains about harassment, there are probably two, or four, or perhaps eight more who were harassed but did not complain. This point of view is quite different from the one organizations usually get. More typically, when managers encounter an allegation of sexual harassment, they may want to find out first how such a problem was handled in the past. If there were no or only a few previous recorded complaints, one understandable conclusion is that the current allegation is a fluke: "It was a misunderstanding," "she is too sensitive," or "she is a troublemaker."

On the basis of relatively few prior complaints, managers can easily conclude that harassment is virtually nonexistent. Since it is virtually nonexistent, then the woman making the complaint must be the problem, and if the incident leads to a court case, the organization invariably offers what I call the "crazy woman defense." In essence, they try to show that it is her fault: She is imagining the whole thing, she is a troublemaker, she has severe emotional problems. In short, she is crazy. From management's official view of the situation, one dramatic court case against a background of no formal complaints, the "crazy woman" charge seems sensible. It is less sensible from the perspective of this research showing that sexual harassment is a sizable problem in the workplace, that the vast majority of harassed women do not make formal complaints, and that women are concerned both about their own career future and the career of the harasser. From this perspective, one might more rationally view a formal complaint as the "tip of the iceberg"—an indication of problems in the workplace, not an indication of a problem woman. This point of view is likely to lead first to attention to the woman's complaint and second to an investigation of the events. The actions implied by this point of view are likely to keep the conflict from escalating to a court case.

In making an investigation, knowing that harassers tend to approach more than one woman can be useful. The women on the job often know the men who constantly make passes at women. In several universities, for example, I found that women students knew the names of professors who habitually try to seduce their female students. Sometimes, women view the man's behavior as harmless idiosyncrasy, or an outgrowth of his personality ("he's like that—a real touchy person") or some circumstance ("he's going through a difficult divorce"). More frequently, the women are much more negative about the person. "Creep" and "jerk" were the most popular labels used by women in the survey.

Furthermore, because these men relate to women workers as women rather than as workers, they may be wasting valuable work time—both their own and the women's. In addition, if they supervise the women they harass, they are probably not making effective use of them as employees (for as long as the women remain on the job). The man who is looking for a potential sexual partner when he hires a secretary will probably not get the most effective secretary. And the sales manager who is eager to have sex with a female member of the sales staff may spend lots of time with her, but whether he is helping her be a better salesperson is questionable.

FIVE

Workers' Reports of Sexual Overtures

Although Chapters Three and Four emphasized the problem of sexual harassment, the most common kind of sexual interaction at work is unlikely to be considered harassment by either party or by their organization. Sexual comments intended to be complimentary were more common than any of the other behaviors studied. Even some of the more serious behaviors—sexual touching, for example—were often encouraged by men and were not perceived as problems by them.

Moving back to the broader perspective of sex at work, this chapter covers workers speaking about their own experiences, concerns, and problems. Not surprisingly, their concerns were not always identical with the research agenda. Working people in general tolerate all kinds of behavior at work. Some clearly offensive and nonprofessional behavior is shrugged off, attributed to the idiosyncrasies of the offending party. Joking and kidding are another theme that recurs in people's comments. Sexual behavior, masked as a joke (as in "we were just fooling around"), is common at work. Power, masking as sex, is also common.

Workers also discuss sex as a commodity. The people in the survey reported some cases of people offering sex in exchange for rewards and, perhaps even more often, offering organizational rewards in exchange for sex. Finally, providing corroborating data for the findings reported in the past two chapters, comments by women and men stress different themes. Women's comments were more likely to tell how men use sex to display dominance and power. They also commented on being sex objects and the extent to which the same men make passes at "anyone wearing a skirt." The men, on the other hand, were more likely to describe dating relationships and normal business interactions.

All of the quotes in this chapter are from the group of men and women who said they had experienced at least one of the following from an opposite-sex person at the current job or any previous job: sexual touching, dating or socializing as a job requirement, and sexual activity as a requirement of the job. All workers who had such experiences were asked to comment on them; not all respondents did so. Some preferred not to comment or cited a lack of privacy to discuss the matter. Others gave noncommittal or uninformative comments. Nevertheless, the number and diversity of comments were substantial. Thirty-eight percent of the women (318 women) reported one or more of the three experiences just listed, and 281 provided meaningful comments. Thirty-six percent of the men (147 men) reported one or more of the experiences, and 122 of them provided meaningful comments.

Sex at Work

The existence of sex at work is clearly and consistently documented in the comments of working men and women. Workers report both flattering and insulting experiences.

Mutually Entered Social-Sexual Experiences. The forms of sexuality reported by working men and women vary; some experiences are mutually entered and mutually enjoyed. At one extreme, some people reported incidents that involved a spouse or intimate friend. For example, one man reported: "The person and I were close friends. I think she was letting me know how she felt. . . . I didn't think much of it except that I usually do the touching." Another man added, "It was my girlfriend and it was OK with me." And one woman said, "We were good friends and I guess he thought that was the thing to do. I guess he felt like it." In response to why the incident occurred, another woman said, "Because he was my husband. I work with my husband."

Other responses were not as clearly mutually entered but they were clearly flattering to the recipient, and a relationship developed. The analyses presented in Chapter Three show that such comments were made more frequently by men than by women.

> We were at the lunch desk. I was contacted under the table. She stepped on my foot. That told me that she was interested in sexual relations. Fast contact. Then we talked about things and started dating.

> Man meets woman. Just working and they get off on their breaks and talk and after three or four months you either make it or you don't. Just from talking. She starts telling you about her problems and you start telling her about yours and then you wind up in the sack. She has problems with her old man and says she doesn't have any sex at home and you start saying the same and pretty soon you say we should do it together.

Finally, some open-minded responses indicated that the respondent was flattered by an overture, but it did not lead to a relationship.

> I work in a uniform. Men in uniform seem to attract women. I work in a medical clinic. I was discussing a patient and the woman touched me. She touched me between the legs. It was shocking to me because I am old-fashioned. Being a man, I never complain. I am flattered or basically shocked when this sort of thing happens.

> It had to do with a pair of pants I was wearing. He thought they were nice. He smacked me on the rear end. We all laughed.

Sexually Harassing Experiences. At the other end of the continuum were reports of clear sexual harassment, many of which resulted in the respondent quitting the job. Many women but none of the men reported quitting a job as result of an incident they discussed in the interview. This is consistent with information presented in Chapters Three and Four: few men have quit a job because of sexual harassment. In this study, only 4 of 405 men reported quitting a job because of sexual harassment (and none of them mentioned the experience in response to open-ended questions about a specific incident). None of the men mentioned either that they were fired or that they appealed to others for help in handling the incident. One man did mention that he fired the offending woman: "I really don't know why [it happened], except that she was a poor worker and probably thought this was a way to get out of work. I fired her, she filed a grievance against me for harassing her, and I filed a counter suit, which I won."

In contrast to the men, many women reported that they had quit jobs as a result of harassment. Some common themes run through their accounts:

> I was complaining to him about other men and he told me not to pay any attention to them and go out with him. So I quit.

> I was young and it was an older person. Because I was only a teenager he thought he could get away with it. The only weapon I had was to quit.

> Many club owners try to wield their power by demanding sexual favors from women. It's the old Hollywood syndrome that's comparable to the casting couch. Many of the females go for it. I've quit jobs because of this demand.

> It was just the type of boss he was. He was a gross man. That was his manner toward everyone in the office. He thought it was cute that he could have every woman in the office. He was executive vice-president and he thought this would give him special privileges. I thought it was disgusting how he acted. He acted real macho, like he was God's gift to women. I quit.

> He was totally sick. He had made previous attempts on other women. His hands all over you. I sometimes had to struggle to get away. He kept

thinking I would give in to him. I finally had to quit the job.

In the majority of cases where one of the two people departed from the job, women reported that they left, but in three cases the man involved was fired, transferred, or left the organization.

> [It happened] because the guy was a drip. He was a salesman with an overinflated ego. He thought he was marvelous. He thought everyone was free game. He wasn't very happy. He had been married three times. He was fired from his job.

> He did it to everyone. He was just "handsy." He was transferred because of it.

> He was a real jerk, and maybe I did something to bring it about, but without knowing it—unintentionally. He was wobbling all over the place with his hands all over us, especially if you happened to be in a room by yourself. It happened a few times with me and others. Basically, he would pin me up against the wall and it was very embarrassing. It happened a lot and he tried it with other females and he finally wasn't employed there.

On the other side, in the course of discussing incidents, some women said that they were fired. For example: "I worked at another restaurant. [I was] asked by the owner to go out and refused three times and was fired."

These quotes corroborate the analyses reported earlier, showing that a sizable minority of workers (more women than men) suffer negative consequences from social-sexual incidents at work. The fact that so many women simply leave work suggests that at work, as in other situations, women are responsible for setting the "moral tone." They are also responsible for handling any sexual situation that might arise, a point that was demonstrated in Collins and Blodgett's (1981) study of managers. The fact that women are sexually harassed represents—to them and to their organization—a failure on their part to communicate the proper moral tone. Thus, they have the option of quitting, which also may be acknowledgment of failure to control the situation.

Many other women reported instances that would generally be considered sexual harassment, but they did not quit their jobs and the offending men were not removed from the workplace. The resolution of these overtures, which were clearly offensive to the female recipients, is not always obvious from their comments.

> Because this man went after every girl in the office and he went after me. Every female who worked in the office was subjected to this guy. We got fired if we did not go out with him.

> Because he was a creep. He was my supervisor. He was just one of those people. That's all that's on his mind. It happened to other women, too. Thank God there aren't that many like him. I fixed him. I spilled hot soup all over his lap later.

> Well, he was supervisor and was like that with all the young girls, putting his hands where they don't belong.

> I was younger. He was a wolf and came up and rubbed against me. I told him what I thought of him and told him what I would do if he ever tried it again.

> It's a touchy question. I think he wanted to prove himself to me. So I would see him in a different light. He always wanted me to go out with him. He cornered me in the cloak room and that's about it. I was afraid and didn't say anything about the situation.

Sexuality as a Joke. Some of the findings in Chapter Three suggested that sexuality is often cloaked in humor. The phrase "fooling around" suggests play and humor, yet, when one's spouse is "fooling around" with someone else, it is rarely a laughing matter. The following comments illustrate workers' evaluations of expressions of sexuality that are interpreted as kidding or joking rather than real sexual expression.

Several men interpreted women's overtures as "kidding around," for example:

> Just joking around. The situation at work is like one little family. It's just part of the game. Everybody does it. When you work the hours we do, early A.M., late P.M., you're tired and you joke around. We practically live together.

> It's hard to say. We were just sort of joking. I never made it with her. We were just sort of joking around. She was married so I would never go out with her. Basically, it just happened because we were joking around. Society today is a lot freer than in the older days. Human nature has always been the same. She still writes me. She was friendly, not in a "trampy" way.

> We were horsing around. No big deal. She touched me on my penis. It was all in fun.

> She pinched me. It was just in fun. We were good friends. I asked her to go out and I was kidding. Then she accepted.

Women also frequently interpreted men's advances as not serious, as joking or kidding around.

> Just in a joking sort of way. It was not really serious. He is a very young man and I think he was just joking or playing around.

> There were a lot of men where I worked. A lot of horseplaying.

Some of these women do not seem to be angry at the harassers, even though they describe incidents that some respondents would consider sexual harassment.

> It was more kidding than anything else. It was a tease, playing. It was done to show other people he could do it. I'm used to it.

He put his arms around my waist. He touched
everywhere. He was only kidding. I know him and
that was the way he was.

Presumably, these are the reactions of a small minority of women
since most women who experienced the more serious social-sexual
behaviors reported feeling anger and disgust (discussed in Chapter Four).

Whether the incidents these people described should be
considered serious or not, sexual or joking, is unclear. It is clear
that when people interpret an overture as "horseplay," "joking,"
or "kidding around," they do not seem to be upset. Kidding
around at work is acceptable behavior to many working people,
even if it means being touched "everywhere."

Sexuality as Normal Work Behavior. Some people view sexuality as a normal part of work behavior. For example, one man
was almost vehement in asserting the normality of sexual behavior
at work: "I think it's pretty normal. Period. I think it's a normal
thing!" Other men claim that although it might not be desirable
or "normal" behavior, sexuality exists and is often a part of the
job. On reading their comments, one might conclude that some
of them may have been describing legitimate work-related, asexual encounters with female colleagues. For example:

It was a social situation. It was sort of a requirement. Sort of escort thing. It was business
related.

It was part of the job. Had to make calls with
her to customers' offices. No social thing.

It was part of the job in the real estate business. We just go to do the job.

None of the women reported similar incidents. It is possible
that these men were discussing cases of working together with a
woman or attending a business-related social affair along with a
female colleague. These men responded affirmatively to the following question: "Sometimes on the job, a woman expects a man
to go out with her with the understanding that it would hurt his

job situation if he refused, or would help if he accepted. . . . Have you ever been asked by a woman to go out with her as part of your job?" None of the women who responded affirmatively to a similar question described routine business meetings, meals, or conferences with male colleagues, yet apparently several men interpreted this question in that manner.

It is also possible, of course, that these men do view work-related interaction with women as sexual as well as work related, even though other people do not think these interactions are sexual. (See, for example, Chapter Three, showing that the experiences of men were less likely to be labeled sexual harassment than were experiences of women.) Gutek, Morasch, and Cohen (1983) found that men were more likely than women to label several sexually ambiguous interactions between the sexes as sexual and that men were more likely to label such behavior as normal work behavior.

Sex as a Means to an End. One of the factors that emerged strongly in the comments of the respondents, but was not a focus of the research project, was the extent to which people use sex to receive privileges or favors. Both men and women reported numerous incidents in which the opposite sex wanted special privileges. At least, the respondent interpreted the other's behavior in that way. Some comments from men:

> Because she wanted privileges, time off. Coming in late, things like that; job-related privileges.

> I think she was trying to fish for a better grade. I felt something like that was going on so I pretended not even to notice. That was it. Nothing further was attempted. It was an obvious trouble area to stay away from.

> Looking for a promotion. Trying to get in good with the boss.

> The woman in question thought she could get what she wanted from me so she came on to me. In my position, I meet women all day and it is not uncommon for them to proposition me.

Women are not as frequently in the position where they could grant favors or privileges to men, but there were a few reports by women in such a position:

> Oh, I think he was someone who worked for me and I think he meant it as a compliment, and he thought it would make his job more secure.

> I think the person thought it would help his job more favorably. He was in a lower position and thought it would enhance his job.

In terms of sex as a means to an end, what women frequently report that men do not is the man's promise of rewards for her if she will comply with his requests. Thus the man offers the woman an opportunity to use her sexuality in exchange for an organizational reward she desires such as a promotion. Some examples:

> A very aggressive male personality. Was just a macho thing. Ego. Type of person. Inferred it would help me in my job. Just a domineering male type.

> Because the situation permits it. Because you're a woman. Because he's the supervisor, you're the subordinate. The pressure. Play or don't get your promotion. Far too much of this going on.

> Well, I was sixteen, working at a taco place. We had a manager, he was that way with all the girls. The only reason I got the job was he wanted to go out with a friend that was working there and said if she would go out with him he would hire me.

> I don't think I can say what motivated it. We had been just good friends. It was a supervisor. At the time he had been lonely. He had left his wife. He had been physically attracted to me for some time. It happened after work and he said it would help my job situation if I accepted, that I would move up. I didn't accept.

Finally, one man made a more general statement about workers "using" sex on the job: "Our business is not just in the office in the real estate business. A great deal of young people use sex as a tool to conduct business. We don't encourage or condone it."

These comments suggest that some workers of both sexes are willing to trade sex for organizational rewards and that some people think that offering organizational rewards will motivate their subordinates to become sexually involved. The question remains: Does it work? Do people advance when they become sexually involved with a supervisor? Is sex a useful commodity for exchange?

None of the men reported that they received a promotion or special privilege for having sex with a female supervisor, but then only twenty-four men (8 percent of the sample) had female supervisors. In contrast, over half of the women had an immediate supervisor who was male and virtually all women had male superiors somewhere in their organization.

Only one woman suggested that using her sexuality facilitated her work-related goals: "Because I wanted to, women are more vulnerable. This is how I got to where I am today. I'm where I want to be in position at a different job and I no longer have to put up with anything." However, several women reported that they suffered direct negative repercussions for going along with the man's proposition. For example: "I was young and foolish. He was older and the boss. It ended with my getting fired."

All in all, there is little evidence from this study that willingness to engage in sexual or flirtatious relationships with supervisors is a useful strategy for advancement. The U.S. Merit Systems Protection Board's (1981) study of federal employees also found that few people benefit from sexual liaisons with colleagues or supervisors. It seems likely that when a supervisor offers a reward to an employee or when an employee offers to become sexually involved with a supervisor, the actual rewards are very small. They might involve leaving work a little earlier, getting a nicer desk or typewriter, receiving extra help at work, and the like. People do not receive substantial promotions, larger salaries, or more responsibility. And certainly no one ever "sleeps" their way to the top.

Differences in Comments by Women and Men. An examination of the open-ended comments of workers reveals that women and men emphasize some different themes. Of the six areas of difference, four are emphasized by women. First, women are more likely than men to cite the initiator's need for power or wish to dominate. The harasser's desire to dominate women is a common theme in women's comments but exceedingly rare in men's. Second, women are more likely than men to mention that the initiator viewed them as sex objects rather than as individuals. Another difference is that some women blame themselves or women in general for eliciting overtures from men, whereas such comments from men are rare, although men more frequently admit some responsibility for an overture from the opposite sex. The largest difference, discussed earlier, is that women are likely to say that the male initiator approached many women. These women felt they were not singled out by the man; rather, they were one of many targets. As one woman expressed it, she was "merely next in line."

Men, on the other hand, were more likely than women to report that the initiator liked them and that friendliness or attraction led to the overture. Finally, a number of men described incidents that sounded like normal work-related interchanges without any sexual component at all. None of the women's comments described such nonsexual encounters.

Although men were not likely to mention power or the need for power in their comments about their experiences, women did so frequently. Sometimes they mentioned the man's position of power or his need for power; other times they cited their own lack of power. Some examples:

> He felt that he was the boss and any new girls that came in, he wanted them. He knows that he is the boss and a big man and he's going through that stage where he felt he had to ask every new girl out. I discovered him right from the start and I think he got the idea that I was not going to go out with him or listen to that kind of bull.

It was a take-advantage-of-a-young-girl situation. He asked me out on a date and then the overtures, and then stronger. He was my boss. He was
in his forties. I was twenty-five.

I get the feeling they think they have the lee-
way to do this because I'm only a secretary.

Women were more likely than men to report that they were
treated as sex objects. The woman symbolized sexuality and it was
that sexual symbol, not the person, that elicited an overture from
the man.

I don't know, because they . . . they think it
is cute and clever and this is their way to relate to
females. For this reason: Some men relate to women
as sex objects or toys; that's the way they relate to
women.

Because the man thought it was his right to
go after me. I worked with some very chauvinistic
men. They thought women were sex objects. They
would make sexual jokes and I was expected to respond to the jokes in a favorable way or else they
would call me a dyke or lesbian.

I think it's because men view women as sex
objects. They think women are only for sexual pur-
pose. This man thought it was a compliment that he
approached me, but I put him in his place. I reported him to the management.

Implied in the concept of blame is the notion that the event
is undesirable. Thus, although some men admitted that they
might have invited or started an interaction with a woman, they
did not blame themselves for the incident and did not blame men
in general for eliciting propositions from women at work. One
comment from a man indicated responsibility but relatively little
blame: "Because I bring it on myself. The clothes I wear. Leave
them open. That sort of thing."

Women, however, occasionally blamed themselves for the

incident they reported or blamed women in general for eliciting overtures. Some examples:

> Because I was looking for a father figure. It was my fault. Anything that happens to you is a subconscious need of yours.

> Because I was standing too close to him while talking about work.

> Oh, I probably had on a dress that made this man want to pat my back.

> Well, we are close employees and it happens frequently. Women are gross and more aggressive than the men.

The amount of self-blame women reported was substantially less than the amount of blame attributed to the initiator (as demonstrated in Chapter Four; see also Jensen and Gutek, 1982). Presumably one reason the initiator was blamed was that he frequently harassed many women. Thus, his behavior was consistent with female colleagues, a situation, according to attribution theorists, in which respondents should attribute causality to the initiator. Indeed, in this study, the single distinguishing characteristic of male initiators found in Chapter Four was their proclivity for making overtures to women at work. The comments of women recipients support this finding:

> Because the man was prone to do it. It didn't make any difference who it was. He had a problem. He just tried to touch anyone whenever he had a chance.

> Testing to see what would happen. I made it clear it better not happen again. He thought he was a killer. Tried it on all the women.

> He's a horny old man. He tries it on everybody. He tries to hold you around the waist tight and kiss you.

> The owner is always coming up and hugging me and patting me on the butt. He does it to the other girls, too. He's always done it. I don't even think about it. He's affectionate. It's a very friendly thing.

> The type of person he is, he asks everybody. Whatever he can get, he'll take. He asked to give me a back rub. I said no. He said I didn't trust my own sexual feeling.

Even when women reported serious sexual attacks, they often mentioned that the initiator had approached or attacked other women. For example: "I was young and innocent, a junior in high school, and was unaware. It was my first job, as a waitress, in a resort. It was family owned, and they helped me. The young man broke into my room and tried to rape me. He tried to do this with other girls. He was college age."

In contrast to the women's comments, the men's comments had relatively few consistent themes. The most frequent idea in the men's comments was that the woman's overture was an expression of affection, friendship, attraction. Some examples:

> I think she liked me. I was young and she was married. She wasn't very happy with her husband.

> There was this little blond who had the hots for me.

> We were talking and I was joking around, sort of flirting, and she came up to me and pinched me. I had heard she supposedly liked me (one of my friends told me). She always came around and we started to get closer and closer.

> I don't know. Physical attraction. Maybe she was turned on by me. I don't know. Maybe she was easy.

> We were just good friends and we had a date. We went out to dinner and drinks. She just liked me.

I treat them good. I'm friendly. I treat them decent
and nice. She was nice and friendly.

Some of the men's comments seem to describe events that,
if the actors were the same sex, would not be described as sexual
at all. These events, mostly meetings or meals, appear to be or-
dinary everyday interchanges that might involve two men or two
women but, in this case, involve a man and a woman. Each of the
following comments was made in response to questions about sexual touching, required socializing, or required sexual activity:

Because we needed to talk about something
related to her investments. It was strictly a business
luncheon; no hanky-panky.

Was caused by just something someone said,
like, "How would you like to go out with him?" And
she put her arm around my shoulder and said "I
wouldn't mind." It was just in a joking way—a kidding manner.

It was part of the job. Had to make calls with
her to customers' offices. No social thing.

Summary

What is sexual? What are the limits to the expression of
sexuality? These are two of the issues that emerge from this project. Some of the comments made by workers did not appear to
be sexual. Other comments that appeared to be sexual harassment
were accepted by the recipient who did not view them as explicitly
sexual (but who, nevertheless, reported them to the interviewer).
This seems to be true especially when the recipient interpreted
the behavior as kidding or joking.

These puzzling reports led to a study designed in part to
understand the conditions under which behavior is considered
sexual (Gutek, Morasch, and Cohen, 1983). One of the findings
of that study was that men were more likely than women to label
any given behavior as sexual. Thus, a normal business lunch seems
to be labeled a "date" by some men just because the luncheon

partner is a woman. On the other hand, a pat on the fanny or a hug and a kiss may not be viewed as sexual by some women because the initiator is "just joking" or is homosexual. Gutek, Morasch, and Cohen (1983) also found that men were more likely than women to view any specific sexually ambiguous incident as appropriate work behavior.

A study by Abbey (1982) provides corroborating data. She showed that what a woman intends as friendliness may be interpreted by a man as a sexual overture. These open-ended comments from respondents suggest that some men attribute women's sexual overtures to friendliness. Abbey's (1982) study lends credence to the interpretation that some sexual overtures motivated by friendliness were not intended by the women to be sexual at all, but were merely friendly gestures.

One interpretation for the broad range of comments elicited by questions about sexual touching, required dating, or required sexual activity is that the questions were too ambiguous and broad, that they could easily be understood to include nonsexual interchanges. Certainly, the questions were intended to elicit a wide range of comments. For example, the phrase "sexual touching" was used intentionally because it is vague. The question about being required to "go out" with a person of the opposite sex is also vague.

One reason for asking the open-ended questions was to find out how people interpret the questions about sexual touching, required dating, and required sexual activity. Although it is possible to interpret a question about required dating as a question about nonsexual, work-related meetings or meals, it is unlikely that many people interpreted it this way. Ninety-one percent of the surveyed men and 96 percent of the women said that being expected to "go out" was sexual harassment (see Chapter Three, Table 1). Perhaps a small percentage of men, less than 9 percent, view any interchange with a woman as sexual although not inappropriate.

In response to the question about sexual touching, 58 percent of the men and 84 percent of the women said sexual touching was sexual harassment. This gender gap appears to be attributable to the two findings mentioned earlier: (1) men describe more events as sexual so that their repertoire of sexual touching is much broader than women's, and (2) men view sexual events as more appropriate than women do. For some men, patting a female colleague or subordinate on the fanny is acceptable behavior. But the woman whose fanny was patted might describe the incident as sexual harassment.

The open-ended comments in this chapter reveal the wide range of workers' experiences and flesh out the statistical analyses presented in the previous two chapters. They also suggest that workers vary in their underlying assumptions, values, and attitudes about sexuality at work. We do not all share the same perspective on sexuality at work, which makes it difficult to gain a consensus on how to handle the problem or even whether a problem exists. The next chapter examines workers' attitudes and tries to account for some of the variation in them.

SIX

Women's and Men's Attitudes About Sexuality in the Workplace

The preceding three chapters focused on people's experiences and their behavior, with a particular interest in the problem of sexual harassment. We now know that it is a common problem at work but that other, nonharassing sex is even more common. Why should something that occurs so frequently and is experienced as a problem fairly often be so invisible? My first hypothesis concerns people's attitudes. Maybe people think sex at work is good, enjoyable, and welcome. Maybe their attitudes toward sex at work are considerably more favorable than many of their own experiences.

Little is known about workers' attitudes about sexual overtures at work. There are even relatively few myths or stereotypes relevant to this issue. The stereotype that women went to college to find husbands was prevalent in the past, but the view that women found jobs to find husbands was less common. (Although some of the promotional material encouraging women to enter clerical and secretarial work in the 1950s and many movies from that decade seemed to present the possibility of marrying one's boss as the ultimate reward of the job.)

Perhaps the most common relevant stereotype is that some women are willing to use their sexuality to advance and thus gain

Table 1. Relationship of Sex of Respondent to Response to Proposition from
an Opposite-Sex Worker.

	Male Respondents (N = 393)	Female Respondents (N = 814)
How would you feel if asked to have sex?		
Flattered	67.2%	16.8%
"It depends"	8.9	14.4
Insulted	15.0	62.8
Neither, it wouldn't happen	8.9	6.0
	100.0%	100.0%

an unfair advantage over men competing for the same job. Some of the people in this study expressed this concern, although I found virtually no evidence that women benefit in this way. Nevertheless, this belief may lead some people to attribute any advancement by women to their willingness to "put out." An intriguing newspaper account reported that male coal miners believe that women who take mining jobs are "looking for sex." These stereotypes assume that women encourage and welcome sexual advances from men.

Note that these stereotypes are about women only. Comparable statements about men—that they "sleep" their way to the top or get jobs to find wives—are exceedingly rare. Although some people might believe that women use their sexuality as a resource at work, apparently few believe men do. To date, none of these beliefs has been studied empirically. There is little evidence that either a majority of workers or certain segments of the labor force hold such beliefs.

We do not even know people's attitudes toward sexual overtures at work. Do most people think overtures are flattering or insulting? Do men think women are flattered by their advances? Do women think women are flattered by men's advances?

The Giant Gender Gap

The biggest gender gap found in this study does not have to do with people's experiences or with their definition of harassment; it has to do with their attitudes and reactions to overtures from the opposite sex. Table 1 shows that 67 percent of the men in the Los Angeles County survey said they would be flattered by a proposition made by a woman at work, but only 17 percent of the women said they would be flattered by a proposition from a man. Whereas most women said that sexual advances are insulting to them, only a minority of men apparently feel this way—a giant gender gap.

What makes this finding so astounding is that neither men nor women are aware of this gender gap. Both sexes are aware that men are flattered if a woman propositions them, especially if she is attractive. Men strongly agree that in general a man is flattered if an attractive woman at work propositions him. Women tend to agree; they report that men are complimented and flattered by overtures from women, especially good-looking women. What is surprising, however, is that both men and women also report that women are complimented and flattered by advances from a man, especially an attractive man. Although both sexes report that men are more complimented than women, they still report that they believe women are complimented.

It is perhaps understandable that men believe women are complimented—after all, men are. Why shouldn't women be complimented, too? Especially if, for various reasons, women do not directly tell men that they are angered, insulted, or disgusted by male advances, it is possible to understand how men who are not especially sensitive to women's responses might assume that women are complimented. Harder to explain is how women who report that they are insulted believe other women are flattered and complimented.

One possible explanation is that women, along with men, hold the following general belief about women: Being attractive to men is extremely important to women, and overtures and advances are an indication of that attractiveness. This is a variation on the theme that women take jobs in male-dominated fields because they are looking for sex or a husband. Work is simply one of those domains in which a woman's attractiveness can be "validated" by comments, overtures, and advances from men. This general belief asserts the importance of gender over the importance of job for women (see also Feldberg and Glenn, 1979).

If being attractive to men is so important to women, why should they say that they personally are insulted by advances from men? Two reasons come to mind: first, those advances frequently have job-related implications (a lighter or heavier work load, longer or shorter hours) and, second, women want their work, not their physical attractiveness, to be noticed and evaluated. In other words, indications of their sexual desirability are less important than indications of their worth as an employee.

Yet somehow women dissociate their own reactions from their views of other women's reactions. Apparently when an individual woman receives an overture from a man and she finds it insulting for whatever reason, she feels that either she alone responds that way or the circumstances are different for her than they are for other women. For example, she may feel that she did nothing to encourage an advance and is concerned that if she does not act complimented, her circumstances at work will suffer. At the same time, she apparently assumes that when other women receive advances, they must have welcomed or even encouraged them.

Men's and women's responses to other questions in the Los Angeles County survey support this contention. For example, both sexes generally report that both men and women, but especially women, dress to be sexually attractive at work. A somewhat smaller but sizable percentage of people believe that both sexes try to present a sexually seductive image at work, with men more likely than women to endorse that statement.

In addition, a majority of both sexes agreed with the statement that if a man or woman was propositioned at work, he or she could have done something to prevent it. Men thought that women and men were equally able to prevent an advance, whereas women were somewhat less likely to say that women could have prevented a proposition. Similarly, a smaller majority of both sexes agreed with the stronger statement that if a man or woman was propositioned at work, he or she must have done something to bring it about. Again, women were slightly less likely to agree that women who are propositioned did something to bring about the advance.

In general, both men and women in the survey tended to blame or put responsibility on the recipient rather than attribute advances to some nebulous force like sex role expectations. Very few men and women agreed with the statement that sex roles encourage men or women to request sexual favors from others at work, although both sexes were more likely to agree that sex roles encourage men to proposition women. Similarly, relatively few people endorsed the statement that workers who request sex want to dominate the other sex. Women, however, were much more likely to endorse that statement about men than about women. This finding is consistent with some of the comments of women reported in Chapter Five. Some men who make sexual advances to women do so because they "can get away with it." It is one way to "show who's boss," to exert control and domination over another.

Nevertheless, the overwhelming picture one gains from examining people's attitudes about sexuality at work is that most people see it as a flattering, complimentary act in the abstract, and people encourage such advances by dressing to be attractive or even seductive. If advances occur, the recipients probably welcomed them and certainly could have prevented them, had they wanted to.

The one finding that does not fit into this consistent positive picture is women's reports of their own reactions. Women say they are insulted, not flattered, although they think other women are generally flattered and complimented. This intriguing finding leads to two lines of thought.

First, it appears to be a classic case of a group endorsing a stereotype about itself. Other studies have shown that groups believe stereotypes about their own groups. For example, welfare recipients frequently believe that other welfare recipients fit our most negative stereotypes of people on welfare, that they avoid work and are cheating the government. Individually, of course, each welfare recipient views himself or herself as an exception to the stereotype (Briar, 1966). They tend to see themselves as deserving welfare recipients. Similar results have also been found for racial stereotypes (Pettigrew, 1971).

The second line of thought questions women's reactions. Perhaps they say they are insulted but they are really complimented. I can find no compelling evidence why this might be so. If anything, because people are generally consistent in their attitudes, women who believe women in general are flattered by overtures from men should be flattered, too. Their attitudes would then be consistent with the more general beliefs. Men were fairly consistent. If men thought men in general were flattered, they tended to agree that they were flattered. Women were much less consistent.

People may seek cognitive consistency by discounting individual women's reports of not being flattered because they go against the stereotype of women, interested first and foremost in attracting men. That is, when both women and men hear a woman complain about being propositioned, they may discount or deny her reaction: "She didn't really mean that," or "She's really flattered even though she won't admit it." In this study, several women described men who appeared to discount women's own statements. The man, for example, who continues to touch and make comments to women in a department even after they all tell him to stop fits this image. This discounting principle helps to perpetuate myths about women enjoying rape or coercive sex and probably contributes to the general lack of concern about sexual harassment.

In the absence of any evidence to the contrary, I conclude that most women are insulted, not complimented, by overtures from men, but neither men nor most women know this. Both men and women are apparently misinformed about women's reactions to sexual advances by men at work.

Human resources specialists, managers, and counselors who must deal with sex as a problem at work can take a positive step toward avoiding the problem by telling men that women are insulted by sexual advances and overtures. They are not complimented. Because of sex role spillover, some men view women at work the same way they view a lover or wife and assume women like and expect sexual comments. My research shows that they apparently are incorrect in most instances. Most women do not view the workplace as a place to verify or validate their sexual desirability, perhaps because they are too readily seen as potential sexual partners by men at work and too reluctantly seen as serious employees. Women may prefer to direct attention away from their sexuality to help call attention to their work accomplishments.

They may be understandably concerned that when their sexuality is noticed, their work is not. When men make sexual comments, they are interpreted as insults because they draw attention away from work.

Men do not have this problem. In Western society, men are "naturally" viewed as serious workers, and a sexual overture or proposition from a woman does not alter that view of them. Men do not have to worry that they will be accused of using their sex to obtain favors and privileges, or that they only got their job because of their sexual attractiveness. A man can relish an overture from an attractive young woman (the most likely woman to make an overture by men's reports) without having to wonder if she will fire him when the affair is over.

Besides the tendency toward a trade-off in attention between sex and work for women, there is another, perhaps more compelling reason why women are insulted by sexual overtures but men are complimented. For women, sexual overtures more frequently lead to unpleasant negative job consequences, whereas there are few discernible job consequences for men. The past three chapters revealed a variety of negative effects of sex in the workplace for women. A high proportion of working women already have had first-hand experience with sexual overtures and propositions that had many strings attached. The overture may not have been a compliment at all but only the first step in a set of increasingly insistent threats. Many women are rightfully wary of sexual comments and propositions. Women wonder what will happen next, what is expected of them, and how their job is going to be affected. That they can have these concerns while still believing that other women welcome sexual attention attests to the strength of that stereotype about women.

In conclusion, the cluster of attitudes held by both sexes is not consistent with the existence of widespread sexual harassment. The belief that both sexes could prevent overtures, overtly or covertly encourage propositions, and dress to be sexually attractive supports the idea that any social-sexual encounters must be welcome. These attitudes help explain both why sexual harassment was overlooked in the past and why so much documentation has been necessary before people would believe the problem really exists. As people acquire a more realistic picture of sex in the workplace—that it can be a problem sometimes—their attitudes may slowly shift to more accurately reflect reality, which at present is much more complex than people's attitudes.

Origins of Attitudes About Sex at Work

Except for women's personal reactions, the cluster of attitudes people hold about sex in the workplace is consistent and fairly simple. Where did these attitudes come from? What affects them: personal characteristics, individual experiences, the work environment? I surveyed three areas to see how they might relate to workers' attitudes. One is personal characteristics of the workers: education, income, ethnicity, and the like. The second is effects of negative consequences of sexual harassment. People who have personally experienced unpleasant job-related effects are likely to have less favorable attitudes than those who have not. In addition, the ambience of the workplace could influence the formation or maintenance of these attitudes. Organizational ambience refers to the extent to which personal appearance or physical attractiveness is important at work and the sexualization of the work environment.

Personal Characteristics

Education, marital status, occupation, employment status of spouse, presence and age of children, income, ethnicity, and age were examined as possible contributors to attitudes about sexuality at work. The only factor that was somewhat related for men was spouse's employment status. The characteristics of women consistently related to attitudes were education, marital status, and ethnicity. None of these characteristics was as important as the person's gender, which was related to most of the attitudes.

Education apparently has a very liberalizing effect on women's attitudes about social-sexual behavior, but it has no effect on men. The more educated women are, the better able they are to separate work role and sex role, to distinguish goals of work and goals of sexuality, and to appreciate the differential power positions of men and women at work. They seem to be able to avoid sex role spillover.

More specifically, women's education level is related to their attitudes about harassment and women. Highly educated women are more likely than other women to say that they would be insulted if propositioned by a man at work. Whereas 63 percent of the total sample of women said they would be insulted, 69 percent of women who were college graduates and 75 percent of women with more than four years of college said they would be insulted. Not only did they say they would be insulted but they also were less likely to think that other women like being propositioned at work. Women with more education were less likely than other women to think that women who propositioned men want to dominate them and, to a lesser extent, that women who are propositioned caused the overture in any way. Finally, they were generally less likely than less-educated women to think that women dress to be sexually attractive and seductive.

Women's education level was not as strongly related to attitudes about men. In general, more-educated women were more likely than others to think that men act sexy at work and like propositions from women at work. Since women generally underestimated how much men said they liked propositions or acted sexy, these results suggest that more-educated women are somewhat more likely than others to evaluate men the way men evaluate themselves.

Education level of men was not related to any of the attitudes. And although people tend to think that education and income are related, only education showed a relationship to attitudes in this survey.

For women, two findings stand out regarding marital status. First, separated women, who may be most confused about sexual role and work role, are most likely to be flattered by overtures from men and think other women are flattered by propositions at work. Second, the women who are generally most likely to experience sexual harassment—women who are living together with a man or who are divorced—are generally most likely to think that men dress to be attractive or even seductive at work, want to dominate women, and are responding in part to sex role expectations to proposition women. Men's marital status is un-related to attitudes about sex in the workplace.

About 90 percent of the women who had a live-in partner reported that their partner was working, which makes employ-ment status an uninteresting variable for them. However, only 38 percent of the men reported that their partner has a full- or part-time job. Men whose wives were working full or part time were less likely than other men to think that domination plays a role in sexual propositions between the sexes at work.

In general, nonwhite women reported somewhat less tra-ditional values than white women did. For example, blacks and Asians were least likely to think women like being propositioned. Hispanic women were least likely to think that women act sexy at work, while black women were least likely to think women cause or contribute to overtures made toward them. Ethnicity was not related to men's attitudes.

In summary, only a few personal characteristics of women were related to their attitudes: education, marital status, and eth-nicity. In general, women with more education are likely to see men and women as more equally contributing to sexual overtures toward women, whereas less-educated women are more likely to feel that women are responsible for whatever happens. The re-sponses of less-educated women reflect a more traditional attitude in which women are responsible for rebuffing male overtures and setting the "moral standards" by which their relationship operates. Less-educated women tend to see this role for women at work even though women at work have less control over the situation than they might have in a dating relationship. In contrast, the pattern of responses of well-educated women suggests that they are prepared to shift some of the burden for sexual conduct at work from women to men.

Marital status is strongly related to experiencing sexual ha-rassment and other social-sexual behaviors, and the attitudes held by women are generally consistent with their experiences. Women who are divorced or living with a man are more likely to think men try to act sexy at work and like sex of various sorts at work. Separated women, admittedly a small group in this survey, were more likely to report being flattered by propositions and think other women may be flattered, too. Perhaps this group of women is looking for affirmation of their physical and social desirability that is not an issue with other women. Finally, paralleling some other research results, these findings suggest that nonwhite women are somewhat less traditional in their attitudes.

Impact of Negative Consequences of Sexual Harassment

In general, women and men who have experienced negative consequences of sexual harassment have somewhat different attitudes from people who have not personally quit or lost a job because of sexual harassment. For men, having suffered one or more negative consequences of sexual harassment led to viewing both women and men as more often acting sexy at work, that is, dressing to be sexually attractive and even seductive. These significant relationships are necessarily quite strong since so few men reported a negative effect of sexual harassment. Fifty percent of the men who had experienced a negative consequence strongly agreed that women at work act sexy, for example, compared to 26 percent who experienced no negative effects.

A surprising finding is the relationship between suffering negative consequences and being flattered by propositions from women. Ninety-three percent of male victims, compared to 72 percent of those who were not victims, said they would be flattered by a sexual request from a woman at work.

Women who reported negative consequences of sexual harassment were different from other working women in their attitudes about women's role in causing overtures, whether women act sexy, and the role of sex role expectations in men's behavior. In general, women who experienced negative consequences of sexual harassment were less likely than other women to believe that women cause overtures or propositions. Whereas 71 percent of women who had not experienced any negative consequences of sexual harassment agreed that women cause or could prevent propositions, 60 percent of female victims agreed with the statement. Although women victims were less likely than other women to report that women are responsible for receiving propositions, the majority of victims still blamed women.

Like men, women who have experienced negative consequences of sexual harassment tend to think women generally dress
in an attractive and seductive manner at work. Surprisingly, wom-
en victims were not more likely to think that men act sexy at work.

For women, having experienced negative job-related consequences of sexual harassment was also related to believing that
sex role expectations encourage men to proposition women. Sev-
enteen percent of women victims thought sex roles encourage
men at work to request sex from women workers, compared to 9
percent of nonvictims.

Organizational Ambience

Organizational psychologists generally use the concept of
organizational climate to refer to the atmosphere of the workplace
as perceived by employees (see Drexler, 1977). Employees may
perceive one company or one work group as more supportive, for
example, than another. Organizations, departments, and work
groups may vary on many dimensions of climate or ambience. The
term *organizational ambience* is used here to refer to two aspects of
climate (that is, ambience or atmosphere) not previously examined
by organizational psychologists but relevant to the sex role spillover perspective. One is the extent to which personal appearance
is emphasized in the workplace. Some people have jobs in which
their primary activity is to be a sex object. More frequently, if a
woman or man is expected to serve as decoration at work, this is
only one of several aspects of the job.

The second measure of ambience is the extent to which the
work environment is sexualized, that is, there is an ambience that
supports flirtatious behavior, sexual jokes, crude language, and
the like (Gutek and Nakamura, 1982). These aspects of organizational ambience—an emphasis on personal appearance as a prerequisite of the job and sexualization of the workplace—are likely
to affect attitudes about sex at work.

Personal Appearance. In general, both women and men respond the same when they are in jobs where being physically attractive is important. They respond by dressing in a manner that

is attractive and even seductive. Both sexes agree that women and men are more likely to dress to be sexually attractive and present a sexually seductive image when physical attractiveness is an important part of their job. For example, among men who say that physical attractiveness is an important part of their job, 86 percent agree that both men and women dress to be attractive or seductive at work. Both sexes also agree that they are more likely to dress in a sexy manner if either their physical attractiveness or their personalities are important in the way they are treated by the opposite sex. For example, among the women who work in jobs where their physical attractiveness influences the way they are treated by men, 90 percent agree that most women dress in a sexy manner at work. Among men in similar positions, 94 percent say that men dress in a sexy manner at work.

People who work in environments where physical attractiveness or personality is important are generally also somewhat more likely than other workers to think that men and women are flattered or complimented by sexual overtures. These respondents apparently feel that they are being rewarded for being attractive and pleasant and that other people find such reinforcement rewarding. However, the picture is not all rosy. People who work in environments where personal appearance is rewarded, and who then respond with a sexual demeanor, do not necessarily like their work environments. For example, both women and men who work in such environments are not more likely than other workers to report that they themselves are flattered by sexual overtures. In addition, the men (6 percent of the sample) who said their attractiveness was very important in the way women at work treated them were less likely than other men to report being flattered by overtures from women. They were also somewhat less likely than other men to think that men in general were flattered by propositions from women.

Sex in the Office. The extent to which the work environment is sexualized also affects attitudes about sex at work. In general, people who work in sexualized work environments report that employees dress to be attractive and seductive and that they are complimented by sexual advances. Both sexes think women are more likely to dress in a sexy manner in environments where sexual jokes are told frequently. Women also think men are more likely to dress in a sexy manner under those conditions.

Similar findings were obtained for working in environments where people are encouraged to flirt; people respond by dressing in a physically appealing and seductive manner. In environments where either sex is encouraged to flirt, both sexes are likely to implicate sex role expectations. However, men who report that men or women are expected to flirt are somewhat more likely to say that sex roles encourage women to proposition men; under the same circumstances, women say that sex roles encourage men to proposition women.

Respondents who worked in an environment characterized by sexual jokes and comments were generally more likely to report that they and other women and men were complimented by sexual overtures. A similar relationship holds for amount of swearing and being complimented by sexual propositions, especially for men. In general, the more swearing and obscene language in the work environment (much of which has a sexual content), the more men and women report that men are flattered by overtures from women.

In summary, where the workplace encourages sexual behavior, workers respond more favorably to it—at a general level. Since the environment seems to reward sexual conduct, they note that people respond to those rewards and also assume most people like that environment. At the personal level, however, they are less favorable. They may respond to the demands of the environment by dressing in a sexual manner, but are not particularly more flattered by advances made toward them.

Influences on Attitudes About Sex in the Workplace

This excursion into the origins of people's attitudes toward sexuality at work does not really explain where the attitudes come from, but it does show how they are modified. I will first discuss how attitudes are modified and then where they come from, since that is clearly the more speculative venture.

Two broad conclusions can be made regarding influences on attitudes. First, men's attitudes are modified less than women's by the areas examined: personal characteristics, unpleasant job consequences, and the workplace ambience. Second, these areas seemed to modify men's attitudes in the direction of more favorable attitudes but women's attitudes in the opposite direction, toward less favorable attitudes.

Of the personal characteristics that would be expected to modify attitudes, education clearly stands out. Education, in general, might be expected to facilitate cognitive complexity and the ability to deal with abstractions. The more education women have, the more they are able to see sex in the workplace as a complex, many-sided phenomenon, with both positive and negative aspects. Educated women were less likely to think that women like being propositioned at work, less likely to think that women caused the overture in any way, and more likely to think that men act sexy at work. Yet, education did not modify men's attitudes at all.

Experiencing negative consequences of sexual advances modified women's attitudes again in the direction of more negative, complex attitudes. They blamed women less and expectations associated with male sex roles more. Since most men did not have negative job consequences, they could not modify their attitudes much. Experiencing negative consequences of sexual harassment made men more likely to endorse the statements that women dress in an attractive and seductive manner at work.

The work ambience likewise affected men and women. The more important physical attractiveness was in their work and the more sexual joking occurred, the more men said they were flattered by sexual overtures from women. In general, these features of the work environment affect the way men view women's reactions. Men tend to think that women act sexy and like advances, too. Women in these circumstances were not more flattered than other women, but they were generally more likely to believe that others like to receive sexual overtures at work.

People's attitudes about sex in the workplace are not assessed often, unlike other areas where attitudes are regularly assessed, such as political preference, attitudes about the economy or foreign policy, and preferences for television shows and consumer products. I do not know of any other attempt to measure attitudes toward sex in the workplace, so whether or not people's attitudes have changed over time is unknown. I suspect that people have not given sex in the workplace much deliberate thought and probably have rarely, if ever, discussed their attitudes with others. Many people in this survey may not have had a conscious attitude until they were asked, for example, whether sex roles in our society encourage men to proposition women at work.

Given this background, it is understandable that people's attitudes are not particularly complex. They seem to reflect two basic beliefs: that the world is just and that sex is fun.

In the absence of other persuasive and compelling evidence—and their own experience seems not to be very compelling or persuasive—people seem inclined to believe that whatever happens to workers is what they wanted or deserved. Thus, if people are propositioned, they must have encouraged it by their behavior and dress and they must like it. If they did not like it, they could have prevented it. The world is just—and simple. Such an attitude dismisses the possibilities of extenuating circumstances like a need to dominate or the subtle but powerful influence of sex role expectations.

Particularly when the "whatever" that occurs is a pleasurable activity like sex (even if it is only a comment or gesture rather than sexual activity), then certainly people must like it and must encourage it. Even though work may not be the most appropriate setting for sexual overtures, what "normal" person is going to reject a little fun at work? Again, this is a simple, unidimensional view of the situation: no acknowledgment that sex is sometimes coercive and violent, that sometimes it is used to control and dominate, that two people do not always feel the same toward each other, and, on a more subtle level, that sex can be used to distract and manipulate others.

Both men and women seem to subscribe to these beliefs even when their own experiences contradict them and even when they have heard of sexual harassment. Eight-five percent of the people in our study had heard of sexual harassment at the time they were interviewed. Yet few people connected sexual harassment with these attitude questions, even those who had been sexually harassed themselves. These attitudes of workers are currently at odds with their own experiences. As more is known about sex in the workplace in all its complexity, its negative as well as positive aspects, people's attitudes may shift to reflect more realistically the complexity of the situation.

These findings about workers' attitudes raise another important question. If people in general think others are complimented by sexual advances and could prevent them if they wanted to, that most people dress to be attractive or seductive to the other sex, is there any reason to think the managers of an organization—most of whom probably are men and claim to feel flattered by overtures from women—will assume otherwise?

On the basis of these attitudes, there is little reason to suspect that sex might be a problem in the workplace. Nor is it particularly surprising, given the limited prior experience with formal complaints, that the initial response to a complaint of harassment is sheer disbelief and the initial official reaction may be to ignore it or label the complainer a troublemaker. Even after an organization has gone through a messy lawsuit, there may be a real lack of understanding of the issue. A lawsuit often makes the organization aware of the threat of lawsuits rather than clarifying the underlying problem. Even after several lawsuits, an organization's management may fail to grasp the dynamics of the problem. Consultants, unfortunately, often play up to this fear of lawsuits by explaining how to avoid lawsuits by following specific features of the law, all the while completely ignoring the problem itself.

SEVEN

How Differing Environments Influence Sexuality

Settings generally convey meanings to the people in them and constrain and shape people's behavior. Being in church shapes one's behavior in certain ways, but being at a football game shapes it in other directions. Some settings convey a sense of formality, others informality. Some settings can encourage sexual display and advances. Certain bars, clubs, and parties, for example, can reduce people's sexual inhibitions. Certain work environments, too, may communicate to workers that sexual comments and overtures are acceptable or even expected of people in that environment.

Sex in the workplace is common and sometimes problematic, but where does it happen? Is sex as a problem equally likely to develop in all workplaces? Is sex equally common in all work environments? That seems unlikely. Some workplaces probably have more harassment, propositions, and dating than others. The ambience in some offices and factories may resemble the ambience of certain clubs or parties.

Workers may be aware of these differences although not particularly outspoken about them. Chapter Four notes that 12 percent of the victims of sexual harassment strongly blamed the atmosphere at work for their harassment. Most of the workers' comments reported in Chapter Five tended to focus on people, not their environment, but some comments reflected their belief that sexuality permeated the work environment. In some departments, secretaries quit regularly because they are uncomfortable with the overtures and jokes. In other departments, supervisors regularly date their subordinates and people seem to change sexual partners with abandon. One man in the survey mentioned that the "young people" in his sales office had affairs with each other and with clients with regularity; he hastened to add that such behavior was not condoned. None of these scenarios is likely to reflect the average work environment, but then little is known about this matter.

This chapter examines characteristics of the workplace to find out which factors are associated with social-sexual activity. The goal is to learn whether some work environments exhibit sex role spillover and whether sex role spillover—strong, marked emphasis on female and male sex roles—is related to sexual harassment and other kinds of sexuality.

This chapter focuses on social-sexual behavior experienced in the job held at the time of the interview because the survey included characteristics of present jobs, not characteristics of previous jobs. Also excluded from the analyses are people's experiences of socializing and sexual activity as requirements of the job because they rarely happened on the current job. Sexual touching, insulting sexual comments, and complimentary sexual comments are analyzed because these three categories reflect various social-sexual behaviors reported relatively frequently by both men and women.

Effect of Sex at Work on Job Satisfaction

Before examining which characteristics of work affect sex at work, let us see whether sex at work affects significant job outcomes such as productivity and job satisfaction. Unfortunately, it was not possible to devise a good measure of productivity for all workers in the survey, but the survey did measure job satisfaction in a standard format. I was able to explore the relationship between social-sexual behavior and job satisfaction. Like most studies of satisfaction (see Gutek, 1978), this one found that most people are very satisfied with their jobs. Only 9 percent of the

men and 12 percent of the women reported that they were dissatisfied with their jobs. These high reports of job satisfaction—
over 90 percent of men and 88 percent of women—are regularly
reported in the literature. Americans consistently claim to be satisfied with all kinds of work.

For men, reports of highly satisfying jobs were not lowered
by their experiences of sex at work. For women, however, they
were; women who were sexually touched or targets of sexual remarks were significantly less satisfied with their jobs than were
women without such experiences. Even experiencing complimentary sexual comments was associated with lower job satisfaction
for women. For example, 6 percent of the women who had received complimentary sexual comments were very dissatisfied
with their jobs; in contrast, only 1 percent who had not received
complimentary sexual comments said they were dissatisfied with
their jobs.

Because so few people were dissatisfied with their work,
the predominant effect of experiencing a sexual advance was to
lower women's job satisfaction from the level of very satisfied to
somewhat satisfied. Thirty-seven percent of the women who had
received insulting sexual comments were very satisfied with their
jobs, in comparison with 51 percent of those who had not received
insulting sexual comments. Being sexually touched had the same
effect; 51 percent of the women who were not sexually touched
said they were very satisfied with their job, whereas only 39 percent of the women who were sexually touched were very satisfied
with their jobs. These results impressively document a general
negative impact at work among women who are targets of sexual
advances, even those intended to be complimentary.

These results fit the general pattern reported elsewhere in
this book. Whatever sexuality men experience has no effect on
their work. They do not quit jobs or get fired; even their job
satisfaction is unaffected. For women, however, the story is different. For them, sex has work-related consequences, including
lowered job satisfaction. Even "nonproblematic" sex, not just harassment, is associated with lower job satisfaction. Any sex at work
affects women's satisfaction with their jobs. These findings are
also consistent with the attitudes of women reported in the pre-

ceding chapter. If women are insulted by overtures from men, it is not surprising that women with those experiences report lower job satisfaction.

Where Does Sex at Work Occur?

Perhaps sex at work occurs only in specific industries, companies, departments, or occupations. While learning the names of companies, occupations, or departments that are hotbeds of sexual propositions and advances may make interesting reading, it is not very useful or constructive for remedying problems and generally making changes. One study that contained such information was not published, and not even the most offending departments were informed of the specific results. The researchers and managers responsible for the study thought that publishing such information would lead to both defensive justification or denials by the offenders and self-congratulations by the exemplary groups but few constructive actions by anyone.

Understanding the kinds of work environments where sexuality thrives is more useful because it provides generalizable information. Knowing that Company A has a lot of sexual harassment is not useful to Company B, but knowing that harassment occurs where there are frequent sexual jokes may help personnel and human resources specialists. This information is useful (1) if it is known and (2) if managers look honestly at their own organizations to see if they have the characteristics of offending work environments. They must anticipate the possibility of a problem developing and take some preventive action.

To understand why sex at work is associated with lower job satisfaction in women, the survey included three characteristics of the workplace associated with sex at work. First is contact with the opposite sex, a necessary but perhaps not a sufficient condition to elicit sexual overtures. Second is an unprofessional ambience, and third is a sexualized work environment. Both the second and third factors relate to workplace ambience. Contact with the opposite sex at work is self-explanatory, but the other two characteristics require some explanation.

Since social-sexual behaviors are, by definition, not work-related events, the environments in which they occur might be characterized by other activities and comments unrelated to work. If the work role is insufficiently defined or separated from other roles, employees may be asked to do activities unrelated to work or treated disrespectfully. The second factor examined in this chapter includes these aspects of work; I call it unprofessional ambience.

Sexualization of the workplace is another aspect of the workplace ambience. This third factor deals with the extent to which female and male roles are emphasized in the workplace and thus is an indication of sex role spillover. Included in this factor are the importance of being attractive and having a pleasant personality and whether men or women are more likely to be hired for the job. In general, being male or female, in and of itself, is not a relevant factor in job performance, and an emphasis on hiring one sex over the other is one indication of an emphasis on male or female roles in the work environment.

Contact with the Other Sex. It is probably common sense to suppose that contact with the other sex is related to amount of sex at work. Of the various people of the opposite sex one can encounter at work, perhaps one's supervisor is most important. An analysis of the effect of a supervisor's gender on workers' reports of sexual activity at work shows a particularly strong effect on women (Table 1). Whether men have a male or female supervisor does not substantially alter the likelihood of experiencing a sexual overture from a woman at work. Although none of the differences is statistically significant, this result is due in part to the skewed distribution of gender of supervisor. In four of the six categories in Table 1, men report more of the experiences when they have a female, rather than a male, supervisor. These findings are relatively unimportant in the current marketplace; female supervisors of men are a rarity. In this study, only twenty-four men have a female supervisor. Should the situation change in the future, it would probably have some impact on the amount of social-sexual overtures experienced by men at work; the same percentages across a less-skewed distribution of supervisor's gender—100 female and 191 male supervisors instead of 24 female and 267 male supervisors—would yield significant differences.

Table 1. Sex of Supervisors by Experiences of Social-Sexual Behavior.

	Male Workers		Female Workers	
	Female Supervisor (N = 24)	Male Supervisor (N = 267)	Female Supervisor (N = 304)	Male Supervisor (N = 408)
Complimentary comments	54.2%	47.0%	39.1%	58.8%
Insulting comments	20.8	13.0	8.9	15.0
Complimentary looks, gestures	39.1	48.9	16.4	56.1
Insulting looks, gestures	13.0	13.1	7.2	10.8
Nonsexual touching	79.2	72.1	62.3	74.2
Sexual touching	30.4	21.1	12.2	18.5

In contrast to the ambiguity in the results for men, the results for women are clear. Five of the six differences are significant. In general, women with male supervisors are more likely to report sex at work, although the supervisor is not necessarily the initiator of the sexual overture. Women who have male supervisors report more complimentary sexual comments, more insulting sexual comments, more complimentary sexual looks and gestures, and more nonsexual and sexual touching, in a comparison with women with female supervisors.

Besides being associated with the supervisor's sex, social-sexual behavior is also associated with contact with the opposite sex. The number of opposite-sex persons on the job is generally associated with sex at work. Men who work with more women than men experience more sexual touching and sexual comments than do men who work primarily with men. Likewise, women who work with more men than women experience more sexual touching and sexual comments than do women who work primarily with women. For example, 11 percent of the women who work with more women than men said they were sexually touched by a man, but 26 percent of the women who work mainly with men said they were sexually touched by a man at work. More women than men work with the opposite sex. Thus, if social-sexual behavior is generally associated with working with the opposite sex, women will experience more social-sexual behavior.

Three other survey questions measured contact with the opposite sex at work: questions about (1) the opportunity for social talking with the opposite sex, (2) the amount of job-related talk with the opposite sex, and (3) the amount of work time spent with the opposite sex. Among men, there is a relationship between talking and working with women and receiving overtures from a woman. Being sexually touched by women at work is strongly related to men's opportunity to talk to women about job-related issues and about social matters, as well as the opportunity to work with women. To illustrate, 10 percent of the men who spend no work time with women said they were sexually touched by a woman at work, in contrast to 30 percent of the men who spend considerable work time with women. Fourteen percent of the men who have no opportunity to talk to women about social matters received complimentary sexual comments from women; over four times as many, 61 percent, of the men who have many opportunities to engage in social conversation with women reported receiving complimentary sexual comments.

Among women, the findings are similar. The more chances women have to work with men or talk to them about work or social matters, the more sexual overtures the women report. For example, 22 percent of the surveyed women who spend a lot of work time with men reported sexual touching, in contrast to 5 percent of women who do not work directly with men. And 66 percent of the women who have numerous opportunities to talk socially with men reported receiving sexual compliments, in comparison with 23 percent of the women who have no purely social interaction with men.

Sheer contact with the opposite sex is related to being sexually touched and receiving both insulting and complimentary sexual comments. Since women have more contact with men at work than men do with women, it stands to reason that women should experience more sexual advances.

Another interesting finding emerged: The harder it is for a woman to get a job, the more likely women in those jobs are to be sexually touched or receive sexual comments. For example, among women who work in jobs that, in their own eyes, are difficult for women to get, 70 percent, compared to 48 percent of other women, reported receiving sexual comments from men at work. Twice as many women who are in jobs that are harder for women to get—22 percent compared to 11 percent for other women—said they received sexually insulting comments from men. Whether men were in a job harder for men to get was not related to the probability of receiving sexual overtures from women.

These findings suggest that some men may be using sex as a way of retaliating against women at work. By making insulting comments and touching women sexually, some men may try to "make life miserable" for the women in those jobs, encouraging them to leave. The relatively high turnover rate among women in some male-dominated blue-collar jobs suggests that this is a successful strategy to force women out. Some comments meant to be complimentary may also have the effect of distracting attention from the women's work and emphasizing qualities unrelated to their work, and while I—and the women in the study—suppose that this is almost always unintentional, occasionally it may be intentional.

Men in jobs that are harder for women to get probably have had relatively little experience with female colleagues and co-workers. Thus, they may be especially susceptible to sex role spill-over. Unsure of how to respond to a woman who is an auto mechanic or a corporate lawyer, men may fall back on the way they respond to other women outside the workplace. If the woman is attractive, they may be especially inclined to make sexual comments, both because they think it is expected of them—by other men and by the woman—and they think the woman will be complimented. While retaliation and sex role spillover seem to happen to women in hard-to-get jobs, they apparently do not happen to men. At least the sexual aspect of sex role spillover does not arise. Other forms of sex role spillover may occur: men may be expected to know how to fix things or assume a leadership position, for example, but men in jobs difficult for men to get do not elicit more sexual overtures or comments from women than other men do.

Unprofessional Ambience. The survey inquired about several activities at work that are generally regarded as inappropriate to a professional work environment. Among them were the extent to which the respondent was treated disrespectfully and expected to do activities that are not formally part of the job and the amount of swearing and obscene language used in the workplace. The workers in the survey were not asked to detail the ways they were treated disrespectfully, but such treatment might include being the target of jokes or insulting comments, being addressed in an insulting manner, being ignored or snubbed by coworkers or supervisors. Similarly, being asked to do tasks unrelated to work can be interpreted differently by different people but might include making coffee, watering plants, washing the boss's car, dusting the furniture, babysitting for a supervisor's children. Finally, obscene language and swearing may be defined slightly differently by various workers. However these three characteristics are defined, they are generally perceived as unprofessional behavior. Some of these unprofessional characteristics of work are related to men's experiences of sexuality at work. Most men do not think they are treated disrespectfully or are expected to do activities unrelated to work. However, 42 percent of the men who were often requested to do tasks not related to work were sexually touched in contrast to 17 percent who never were asked to do such tasks. Sexual touching seems to be a part of disrespectful treatment at work. Forty-six percent of the men who said they were often treated disrespectfully at work also said they were sexually touched at work, but only 17 percent who were never treated disrespectfully were sexually touched at work.

Many more men reported frequent swearing at work, and incidence of swearing was strongly related to experience of social-sexual behavior. The strongest relationship is for receiving complimentary sexual comments: 65 percent of the men who reported frequent swearing at work reported receiving complimentary sexual comments, in contrast to 34 percent who said there was no swearing or obscene language at work but did receive complimentary sexual comments from women.

Among women, those who are treated disrespectfully at work are more likely than others to receive sexual advances. Overwhelmingly, women who said they were never treated disrespectfully also have not been touched sexually; 9 percent who were never treated disrespectfully by their report had been sexually touched. In contrast, of the women who were often treated disrespectfully, 33 percent said they were sexually touched. The results are similar for sexual comments meant to be complimentary. Of the women who said they were never treated disrespectfully, 38 percent received sexual comments meant to be complimentary; 67 percent of the women who were often treated disrespectfully also received sexual comments.

Frequency of swearing and obscene language was strongly associated with women receiving sexual overtures and insults. Seventy-one percent of the women who said swearing occurred frequently at work received sexual comments meant to be complimentary; in contrast, 36 percent who said swearing did not occur at all reported receiving sexual comments meant to be complimentary. Women's reports of sexual touching were over three times as likely in environments where swearing was common than they were in environments where workers did not use obscene language. All in all, sexual advances, including both insulting and complimentary forms, occur much more often in the workplace with an unprofessional ambience than in more professional work environments.

Sexualization of the Workplace. As mentioned earlier, an emphasis on workers' gender in the workplace is generally not necessary for the effective conduct of work; it is probably detrimental to productivity. The extent to which sex is a topic of conversation or men and women are expected to flirt with the other sex indicates the sexualization of the workplace and is an example of sex role spillover.

The survey results show consistently that a sexualized work environment is associated with sexual overtures. Men reported that the more men were expected to flirt with women, the more men received sexual advances from women, but whether or not women were expected to flirt with men had no impact on the amount of sexual advances women made toward men. For instance, the men who reported a lot of social pressure for men to flirt with women were over two times more likely to report being sexually touched than those who said there was no pressure to flirt with women. Of the men who reported some social pressure to flirt with women, 16 percent received insulting sexual comments in contrast to 10 percent who said there was no social pressure to flirt. The relationship is even stronger for amount of sexual talk, which men said was more common than pressure for either sex to flirt with each other. None of the men who said sexual talking or joking was absent from their workplaces was touched sexually or received sexual insults. In contrast, 29 percent of the men who said sexual joking and comments occurred frequently also reported they were sexually touched at work.

Among women, those in work environments with frequent sexual jokes and strong social pressure for men and women to flirt with each other were much more likely than other women to receive sexual advances from men. For example, only 8 percent of the women who said there was no pressure for flirting with men received insulting sexual comments from men, but 27 percent of the women who said there was a lot of pressure to flirt with men received sexual insults. Twelve percent of the women who said men were not pressured to flirt with women were sexually touched, in contrast to 33 percent of the women who said there was a lot of social pressure for men to flirt with women.

Sexual talking and joking were also strongly related to women's reports of social-sexual behavior. Twenty-eight percent of the women who said conversation about sex was frequent were sexually touched, 23 percent of the women who said sexual joking was frequent received insulting sexual comments, and 70 percent of women who reported sexual jokes were common received sexual comments intended to be complimentary. These figures are three to seven times as high as the frequency of these behaviors in environments without sexual jokes and comments.

The extent to which personal appearance and having a "good" personality affect treatment at work or the probability of being hired also indicates sexualization of the workplace. For men, generally a significant relationship emerged between social-sexual behavior and reports that having a good personality affects the way women at work treat them. For example, 31 percent of the men who reported that their personality greatly affects the way women at work treat them said they were sexually touched, in contrast to 13 percent of the men who said personality was not at all important. The same pattern of relationship emerged for physical attractiveness, but the relationships were much weaker. Nevertheless, 40 percent of the men who said their physical attractiveness was not an important consideration received sexual comments meant to be complimentary, compared to 59 percent of the men who said physical attractiveness was somewhat important.

The relationships were much stronger for women. Women who were touched sexually or reported insulting or complimentary sexual comments were likely to say that their personality and physical appearance influenced the way men at work treated them. For example, women who said their personality was an important factor were four times as likely as other women to be sexually touched, twice as likely to receive sexual insults, and twice as likely to receive complimentary sexual remarks. The effects of physical attractiveness were even more pronounced. In general, women, like men, did not think that physical attractiveness was overwhelmingly important in the way men treated them, but the women who thought more emphasis was placed on physical attractiveness reported more sexual advances than other women did. In response to a question about the relative importance of physical attractiveness or personality in treatment by men, women who said that physical attractiveness was more important than personality were more likely to be targets of sexual overtures. For example, for women who said physical attractiveness was more important than personality in the way men treated them, twice as many of them said they were sexually touched and received sexual insults, and one and one-half times as many said they received sexual remarks meant to be complimentary, compared to other women.

Another survey item that dealt with the same issue asked respondents whether an attractive man or an attractive woman would more likely be hired in the respondent's job. Since gender is not a requirement of many jobs, most people could be expected to say that an attractive man and an attractive woman are equally likely to be hired for any given job. And that is what most people said. However, people who indicate that gender is not irrelevant were more likely to report social-sexual behaviors. For example, of the men who said an attractive man is more likely to be hired, 75 percent said they were sexually touched by a woman, in comparison to 18 percent of the men who said gender was not a factor in hiring and 47 percent of the men who said an attractive woman was more likely to be hired. Women who said an attractive man was more likely to be hired received more insulting and complimentary sexual comments than did other women. Jobs for which attractive men are most likely to be hired are associated with social-sexual experiences of both sexes. Jobs in which gender is irrelevant in hiring are least associated with social-sexual behavior.

Overall, the findings strongly support the notion that sex at work is more likely in a sexualized work environment, one in which sexual joking is common, flirtatious behavior is encouraged, people's personality and physical appearance affect the way they are treated by the opposite sex, and an applicant's gender affects hiring decisions. These findings provide support for the sex role spillover perspective.

Conclusions

From the standpoint of the general good of the work organization, sex at work has little to recommend it. It appears to be part of a cluster of unprofessional behaviors and attitudes—an unprofessional ambience—that characterizes some workplaces. One finding from the chapter is worth particular note: Even behavior that might be construed favorably by the individuals involved does not have a positive effect on organizational outcomes. Even sex that is not viewed as a problem—sexual comments meant to be complimentary, for example—has some negative consequences for organizations in the form of lower job satisfaction for women. Although neither the men nor women involved are likely to consider the behavior a problem, and it is not likely to lead to a court case or loss of an employee, sex still has a measurable effect, in the negative direction. The lower job satisfaction that results from sex at work can also affect a woman's productivity, absenteeism, and commitment to work, as the literature on job satisfaction suggests (see, for example, Katz and Kahn, 1978). This is an example of the subtle, unacknowledged effects of sex at work. Neither workers nor managers are aware of them.

Not surprisingly, people who have opportunities to talk or work with the opposite sex report more sexual advances. Sheer contact, in and of itself, is related to men's reports of sexual touching and sexual comments. For women, the nature of the contact with men is also important. For example, women who have male supervisors are significantly more likely than women with female supervisors to report all kinds of social-sexual behaviors.

Chapter Four showed that supervisors did not account for a majority of women's social-sexual experiences, but these findings suggest that even when the male supervisor is not the initiator, he can influence the work climate in a way that encourages or discourages sexual overtures and sexual hostility. Several women in the survey said supervisors ignored or laughed about sexual overtures. In one case where a coworker made sexual remarks to a woman, her supervisor told her she should be complimented. In another instance, when a woman was pinched by a coworker, the supervisor laughed and told her she had no sense of humor. The mere presence of a male supervisor rather than a female supervisor may reduce male workers' inhibitions about approaching women, even though the supervisor may not approach women himself. Men may correctly or incorrectly assume that the supervisor will either condone their behavior or at least ignore it. In the survey, several supervisors made comments suggesting that many do ignore subordinates' behavior, for example, "I wouldn't do that myself, but I figure it's his business."

Men and women who report sexual advances are also likely to report a variety of activities that indicate a general looseness or laxness about maintaining a professional atmosphere at work. These include reports of being asked to do tasks unrelated to work, being treated disrespectfully, and working in an environment where swearing and sexual joking are common, where there is an emphasis on people's personality and physical attractiveness, and where gender is a factor in the way people are treated and hired.

One could conceivably interpret these findings to indicate that the work environments where social-sexual behavior occurs are more relaxed or informal than other work environments. However, that interpretation receives scant support from the research. One of the questions that bear on this matter inquired about the organization's policy about dating between employees: Was it tolerated or forbidden? That question can be interpreted as a measure of informality of policy. In general, the organization's policy toward dating was not related to sex at work. In the few instances where there was a relationship between dating policy and social-sexual behavior, it was in a negative direction, that is, the more sex at work, the less the organization tolerated dating between employees.

Another question that arises in the course of examining the results of this chapter concerns the meaning of a "good" personality. The survey questions are much more general than the way psychologists usually address the issue of personality. Men and women both reported that when having a good personality influences the way the opposite sex treats them, they are especially likely to be sexually touched and receive sexual comments. What do they mean? One possibility is that they respond to the question about the importance of personality by making an implicit comparison between task requirements (such as ability to manage people, type, or operate a lathe) and peripheral characteristics (such as personal appearance or personality). Workers may say that personality is important when they feel that personality, or manner of interacting with others, is given more weight than it deserves in comparison with the weight given to their job-related skills and abilities.

This interpretation is consistent with a perspective suggesting that women, more often than men, are noticed and responded to on the basis of attributes irrelevant to the job, for example, their physical attractiveness and personality. Furthermore, attention to attributes unrelated to work is associated with social-sexual behavior. When a man responds to a woman on the basis of her personal attributes instead of her job-relevant skills, he is also likely to make sexual comments or sexually touch her. Likewise, when a woman responds to a man on the basis of his personality instead of his job-relevant skills, she is also likely to direct sexual remarks to him.

Although the process may be parallel for the two sexes, the effects are greater for women because women are more likely than men to report that their peripheral characteristics are given attention. This attention to irrelevant characteristics may also affect women's rates of promotion and advancement. If women's attributes unrelated to work are noticed, it is also plausible that their job-related skills and abilities may go unnoticed or insufficiently noticed, a point that women seem to understand at some level, as was mentioned in the previous chapter.

In addition, the relationships reported in this chapter tend to be stronger for women than for men. Women who come into contact with lots of men or work in a sexualized environment tend to be more likely than men in the same environment to be recipients of sexual touching and both insulting and complimentary sexual remarks. Thus, women seem to suffer more negative consequences than men do from an unprofessional ambience and frequent contact with the opposite sex. No wonder most women say they are insulted by sexual propositions from men.

The results presented in this chapter suggest that some forms of social-sexual behavior that might be construed as positive may not be so positive. Remember that all the social-sexual behaviors studied here occur in the context of work. Perhaps the same overtures from the same people made outside the job—after work or on the weekend for example—might not be as negative. Just because a sexual remark at work has negative job consequences does not mean that the same remark on a date or some other social outing would also have negative consequences. It probably would not. It is the confounding of sex and work, of sex roles and work roles, that leads to negative organizational consequences. The subtle use of sex at work such as making a complimentary sexual remark to a secretary and then asking her to stay late to finish a report may be effective in the short term but much less effective in the long term.

The implications for managers are wide ranging. Professionalizing and desexualizing the work environment are worthwhile goals that should reduce sexual harassment—problematic sex—as well as counter some of the subtle effects of sex at work, like lower job satisfaction among women who are targets of sexual advances. Professionalization and desexualization of work are not just worthy goals for their own sake; they are good for business, for effective work organizations. Managers, of course, can begin by being role models of professional conduct. They can discourage sexualization of the work environment by their own behavior and by suggestions to employees. Managers set the tone for their departments. To a certain extent, they control the ambience of their work group. It is in recognition of the high degree of managerial influence over the work environment that the Equal Employment Opportunity Commission, for example, makes managers responsible for any harassment in their units.

One issue still to explore is whether the sexualized environment is associated with a male-dominated or a female-dominated environment. As was reported in Chapter Two, some of the factors examined in this chapter characterize women's work more than they characterize men's work. These include an emphasis on personality and physical attractiveness. Other factors seem to be more strongly associated with men's jobs. For example, men are more likely than women to report that obscene language occurs in their work environment. The next chapter will explore this issue in more detail by examining the relationships among sex ratios at work, sex role spillover, and sexuality at work.

EIGHT

Explanations for Sexuality in the Workplace: Unequal Sex Ratios and Sex Role Spillover

To examine more explicitly the sex role spillover model, this chapter will tie together a number of themes. Earlier analyses showed that men are more isolated from women at work than women are from men, that women's jobs seem to require physical attractiveness and a good personality more often than men's jobs do, and that contact with the opposite sex and being in a sexualized work environment lead to social-sexual experiences, especially by women.

These results combined with recent findings on sex ratios (Kanter, 1977a; Spangler, Gordon, and Pipkin, 1978; Fairhurst and Snavely, 1983a, 1983b) introduce the idea that a skewed sex ratio at work might be associated with sex role spillover and sexuality at work. Performing a job with predominantly opposite-sex workers is a different experience—and leads to different experiences—from performing the same job with predominantly same-sex workers. This should be true for both men and women,

Note: Portions of this chapter were based on Gutek and Morasch, 1982.

129

although the kind of environment experienced by a solo male is substantially different from the kind of environment experienced by a solo female. That is, male-dominated work environments are very different from female-dominated work environments, and the kind and amount of sexuality are areas of difference.

The impact of sex ratios on sexuality at work has been considered particularly as it would apply to female workers (Gutek and Morasch, 1982). In this chapter, the perspective will be applied first to the women in the Los Angeles County survey because (1) the sample contains more women than men, (2) women experience more sex at work, and (3) their responses and experiences form a more coherent and expected set of results than do the responses of the men in the sample. The same analysis is then repeated with the men in the sample to see if the same line of reasoning applies equally to both sexes.

As mentioned in the first chapter, sex role spillover is a concept used by Nieva and Gutek (1981) to refer to the carryover of gender-based expectations about behavior into the workplace. Being a sex object is one aspect of the female sex role. Findings reported in the previous chapter suggest that being a sex object is more important in some jobs than in others, and here I argue that the sex ratio of the job is a key to whether or not a woman is expected to be a sex object in her work. Before proceeding, it is necessary to clarify and limit the concept of sex ratio.

Sex Ratio

Kanter (1977a, 1977b) brought the concept of sex ratio to public attention through her penetrating analysis of the importance of the numerical composition of a group; she showed how the number of women and men affects the behavior and attitudes of each person in the group. Kanter's analyses focused on small groups, but they can be extended to groups varying in size and boundary. For the purposes of this analysis, three sex ratios are relevant: sex ratio of occupation, of job, and of work group.

The occupational sex ratio of the men and women in the survey was characterized in terms of the percentage of females in the occupation nationwide. Findings presented in Chapter Two (see Figure 1) showed that 61.8 percent of men are in occupations in which fewer than 20 percent of the workers are female; 40.3 percent of women are in occupations in which fewer than 20 percent of the workers are male. Thus the sex ratio of occupation is highly skewed.

Even if the sexes were distributed evenly across occupations, that would not guarantee the elimination of sex segregation at work. An occupation can be sex integrated, but the jobs in a particular organization still could be sex segregated. Some jobs are sex segregated in the opposite direction of the occupation as a whole. For example, there are more waitresses than waiters, but some restaurants hire only waiters. Doctors are more likely to be male, but a feminist medical clinic, for instance, is likely to have only female physicians. Factory workers tend to be male, but minimum-wage factories often hire only female workers. Thus, sex ratio of an occupation is an imperfect measure of sex ratio of a job. One question asked of survey respondents, whether there were more men, more women, or equal numbers of men and women in their jobs, can be considered a measure of a job's sex ratio.

The results presented in Chapter Two suggest that, if anything, classifying respondents by sex ratio of occupation underestimates the degree to which they experience sex segregation on the job. For instance, 42 percent of the women who worked in male-dominated occupations (65 percent or more male workers) said most of the people in their jobs were female. Thus, a substantial number of the women who work in male-dominated occupations still work in female-dominated jobs. Working with equal numbers of same- and opposite-sex workers as colleagues and coworkers is a relative rarity in the labor force.

The extreme sex segregation of occupations and jobs is not always apparent because men and women do work together, but usually in different jobs. Very few women work in an environment without men. The ratio of men to women among the people one works with on a daily basis is also likely to be important and is frequently different from the sex ratio of the occupation or job. Katz and Kahn (1978) use the term *work role set* to designate people with whom one is directly associated at work, usually through

work flow. Here I use the more common term, *work group*, to refer
to this group of supervisors, subordinates, and colleagues. The
work group of a secretary in an engineering firm, for example,
might include a manager, several engineers, several other secretaries, a receptionist, a mail clerk, and assorted others. The work
group as defined here does not necessarily conform to specific
organizational units such as departments, project teams, or divisions; any individual's work group may involve people from other
departments, teams, or divisions. The sex ratio of the work group
affects one's behavior and experiences at work. The sex ratio of
the work group was measured by the question in the survey about
the amount of time workers spend with the opposite sex.

In general, work groups are much less sex segregated than
jobs or occupations. For instance, only 13 percent of the women
in the female-dominated occupations and female-dominated jobs
said they spend no work time with men.

The three types of sex ratio under consideration here can
be ordered in terms of immediacy of impact on day-to-day experiences at work. The most immediate is the sex ratio of the work
group, those people with whom one interacts on a day-to-day basis, followed by the job's sex ratio. Sex ratio of the occupation, the
most remote, probably has the least impact on daily behavior at
work, but provides a context in which work roles may be defined.
The joint effects of all three kinds of sex ratios will be considered
here.

Sex Ratios and Sex Role Spillover

The form of sex role spillover at work is different for
women in male-dominated fields than it is for women in female-
dominated fields. People infuse the work role itself with role expectations pertinent to the sex role of the numerically dominant
gender. Both the worker and others in the role set see these characteristics as part of the job. For example, by definition, cocktail
waitresses are sexy; nurses are nurturant; executives are compet-
itive. Members of the other, numerically subordinate sex are different. Both the majority sex and the minority sex experience sex
role spillover, although of different kinds.

Recent innovative analyses of skewed sex ratios (Kanter, 1977a, 1977b) have tended to focus on the difficulties faced by women who are tokens or solos (Laws, 1975; Northcraft and Martin, 1982; Taylor, Fiske, Etcoff, and Ruderman, 1978). The difficulties faced by women who are the dominant sex at work have not been addressed. Nor have any difficulties associated with being a man in either a male-dominated or a female-dominated group been explored (for an exception, see Etzkowitz, 1971). Further, the research on sex ratio has tended to obscure the distinctions made here among the three levels of sex ratio, either because it uses artificial (laboratory) settings where sex ratio is controlled (Taylor, Fiske, Etcoff, and Ruderman, 1978) or because it has been nonspecific with respect to the details of the setting (Kanter, 1977a). An example of a woman executive in a meeting with all men may or may not be characteristic of that woman executive's routine activities.

Nontraditionally Employed Women. Women in nontraditional work—male-dominated occupations and jobs—experience sex role spillover, spillover that is indirectly related to the numerical dominance of men in their work environments. A high percentage of one sex in an occupation leads to the expectation that people in that occupation should behave in a manner consistent with the sex role of the numerically dominant sex. Male sex role spills over into general work role requirements in occupations numerically dominated by men (and female sex role carries over into general work role requirements in occupations numerically dominated by women). Thus, people in men's jobs are expected to "act like men" to be perceived as good workers. The nature of the sex role and work role is incongruent for the nontraditionally employed woman (and for the nontraditionally employed man as well). When the numerically dominant men expect a nontraditionally employed woman to behave in accordance with their primary conceptions of her—that is, as a woman, rather than as a worker—and behave toward her in accordance with that primary conception, such behavior is often inconsistent with what the expectation would be if it were based on the work role. Furthermore, this expectation based on sex role differs from the behavior expected of other (male) workers in the same job.

Because of these different expectations, the treatment accorded to the nontraditionally employed woman by her male colleagues may be different from the way they treat each other. For example, a woman engineer will be treated differently from the other (male) engineers and part of that treatment is based on the fact that she is a woman. Nontraditionally employed women, by virtue of their jobs, frequently interact with men; that is, their work groups are composed primarily of men. Their numerical rarity makes nontraditionally employed women in male-dominated work (as well as nontraditionally employed men in female-dominated work) distinctive, and it thereby makes their sex a particularly salient characteristic (McGuire, McGuire, Child, and Fujioka, 1978). Numerically dominant men are likely to see these nontraditionally employed women as women first and work role occupants second. They are women in jobs. Further, her sex is a salient dimension to a woman, as well as to her male colleagues, because people pay attention to their own peculiarities, the way they differ from other people in their social environment (McGuire, McGuire, Child, and Fujioka, 1978). Thus, nontraditionally employed women are likely to be aware that they are perceived as different from and treated differently from men in their environment, and this in turn should affect how they experience social-sexual encounters at work. Since nontraditionally employed women are treated as women in jobs, they are probably aware that they are being treated differently from the others (men) in the work role; they will probably believe that this different treatment is accorded to them because of their personal characteristics rather than their work role requirements.

In summary, nontraditionally employed women are treated differently from their (male) colleagues and are aware of this differential treatment. Therefore, in the arena of sex at work, it is expected that these women will be likely to report a high frequency of sexual advances and to feel that sexual harassment is a problem at work.

Traditionally Employed Women. Women who occupy jobs dominated by men are not the only group especially likely to be subject to sex role spillover. Sex ratios also affect women who go into traditional work, that is, female-dominated occupations and jobs. Because a traditional female job is also dominated by one sex, the job itself takes on aspects of sex role. That is, the expectations about the way a traditionally employed woman will behave on the job are similar to the expectations about the way women in general should behave. Whereas women in nontraditional jobs are viewed as women in jobs, women in traditionally female jobs are viewed as women, period. The work role is the female sex role or at least overlaps substantially with it.

Different traditional female jobs emphasize different aspects of the female sex role. For example, some traditional female jobs stress the nurturing aspect of the female sex role, such as jobs in which women interact primarily with children or the sick, aged, handicapped, or poor. The supportive, ego-boosting function aspect of the female sex role spills over into jobs where women are helpers, aides, and assistants such as dental assistants or administrative assistants. The focal aspect of interest here, the sexuality aspect of the female sex role, spills over into jobs in which women are expected to be sex objects—cocktail waitresses, receptionists in some engineering or manufacturing firms, or actresses.

Women workers are likely to be regarded as sex objects when two conditions are met: (1) when the occupation and the job are numerically dominated by women, thereby facilitating sex role spillover and (2) when these women are in work groups with more men who may emphasize the sex object aspect of the female sex role if they wish.

The traditionally employed woman, that is, one working in a female-dominated occupation and job, is typecast by her occupation. She may not notice this typecasting, however, because others in the same job are treated the same. That she is treated as a woman first and as a work role occupant second is not apparent when work role is sex role. It may become apparent to the woman only when the first men are hired for similar jobs—as typists in the secretarial pool for example—and the woman realizes that these men are treated differently from the women in the job (see Schreiber, 1979). Thus, a traditionally employed woman may feel that the treatment she receives reflects her job rather than her personal characteristics. Such woman are likely to describe their jobs as containing aspects of sexuality. However, they are less likely to view and report sexual harassment as a problem at work, because it is "part of the job." These women may report that physical attractiveness is necessary in their work and that flirtatious behavior by both sexes is common at work. In short, sexuality is part of the job.

The Male Situation. The preceding analysis of the female situation rests heavily on the assumption that men tend to emphasize the sexual aspects of the female sex role in their interactions with women at work. In the case of nontraditional jobs for women, men see women as women first, workers second; while they might respond to women in many different stereotypical ways—as their mother or daughter, for example—they prefer to respond to women as potential sexual partners in most cases. In the case of traditional jobs for women, the job becomes "feminized." When most of the work group members are men, the sexual aspect of the female sex role is emphasized in the job over other aspects of the female sex role such as nurturance or cooperation.

Trying to make a case that women prefer to emphasize the sexual aspects of the male sex role is much more difficult. It is not at all clear that women prefer to relate to men at work in a sexual manner over other types of interaction. The findings reported in earlier chapters suggest that they do not. Thus, to argue that men in nontraditional, or female-dominated, jobs have the same problems as women in nontraditional jobs is not convincing. If women are accurately reporting their wishes, that they personally prefer to leave sexuality out of the workplace, then these men may report less sexuality at work than other men with comparable levels of contact with women. All of this may remain speculation: It is questionable whether many men will be in nontraditional jobs as defined here.

A man's gender is likely to be a salient characteristic in female-dominated work just as a woman's gender is a salient characteristic in male-dominated work. However, it is not clear how that characteristic will affect others or if it will contribute to sexuality at work.

Men in traditional work where traditional work parallels my

definition of traditional work for women—men in male-dominated occupations and jobs but female-dominated work groups—
are an interesting case. I assumed that, in the case of traditionally
employed women with male-dominated work environments, men
can emphasize whichever aspects of the female sex role they want.
When traditionally employed men have female-dominated work
environments, it is not clear that women will be able to emphasize
whichever aspects of the male sex role they want. When a woman
works in a male-dominated work group, many of the men she
works with are likely to be supervisors or peers. When a man
works in a female-dominated work group, however, it is unlikely
that most of the women are supervisors or peers, particularly if
his occupation and job are male dominated.

More likely, if the sexual aggressor aspect of the male sex
role is a salient aspect of men's behavior at work, here is where
it should assert itself. In a male-dominated occupation and job,
the work itself should reflect the male sex role, and part of that
role is being a sex seeker or sexual aggressor. If the male sex role
contains elements of sexual assertiveness, then traditionally male
work should include spillover of these aspects of the male sex role,
too. In that case, discussing sexual matters or comparing sexual
experiences may be relatively common in male-dominated work
environments. If so, when men interact frequently with women
in these jobs, they may use the workplace as an opportunity to
approach women in a sexual manner. Another possibility is that,
if sexuality is emphasized, men will interpret their encounters with
women as sexual overtures by women, whether or not a sexual
overture was intended. Yet another possibility is that if sexuality
is heightened in these environments, women will make more overtures toward men than they would in other settings. In any event,
it seems likely that men will perceive more sexuality in their traditional work than in nontraditional work.

Support for the Sex Role Spillover Perspective

Let us now consider findings bearing on the relationship
between sex ratios and sex role spillover. To put these results into
context, five groups of female workers from the Los Angeles

County survey are discussed: those in (1) male-dominated occupation and job, (nontraditional), (2) female-dominated occupation
and job, male-dominated work group (traditional 1), (3) female-
dominated occupation, job, and work group (traditional 2), (4)
integrated occupation and job, male-dominated work group (integrated), and (5) the total sample of female workers.

The five comparable groups of male workers also discussed
are those in (1) female-dominated occupation and job (nontraditional), (2) male-dominated occupation and job, female-dominated work group (traditional 1), (3) male-dominated occupation,
job, and work group (traditional 2), (4) integrated occupation and
job, female-dominated work group (integrated), and (5) the total
sample of male workers.

The Women. Eighty-nine women surveyed (10.8 percent of
the sample) were in male-dominated occupations and jobs such as
architect, manager, history professor, advertising agent, upholsterer, furnace smelter, and sheriff. Fifty-five percent of these
women said they were in supervisory positions, and 81 percent
said they had a supervisor. One hundred women (12.1 percent of
the sample) were in female-dominated occupations, female-dominated jobs, and male-dominated work groups. Among the jobs
frequently included in this subset of working women were registered nurse, bookkeeper, cashier, receptionist, secretary, waitress, flight attendant, and hairdresser. Forty percent of the women
in this group said they were supervisors, and 92 percent said they
had a direct supervisor. Of the 251 women in female-dominated
occupations and jobs, 40 percent of them have male-dominated
work groups. These two groups of women—nontraditional and
traditional 1—should experience sex role spillover. The first
group should be more likely to notice and report social-sexual
incidents.

The sex role spillover perspective implies that women in
integrated work should not be plagued by problems associated
with sex role spillover. A comparison group of women in integrated work was constructed: 100 women working in occupations
that were 15 percent to 85 percent female with equal numbers of
men and women in their jobs. To make this subset comparable
to the other two groups and to control for amount of contact with

men, only the forty-six women in integrated occupations and jobs but male-dominated work groups were selected for analysis. This subset provides a conservative comparison group because only two of the three sex ratio measures display sexual integration. Among the women in this integrated group were a social worker, a designer, an editor, an artist, and several cashiers and postal clerks. Compared to the women in nontraditional work, fewer of these women were in supervisory positions; 45 percent said they were supervisors, and 96 percent said they had a direct supervisor.

Another useful comparison group is traditionally employed women with female work role sets (traditional 2). This group should have relatively few sexual encounters because they come into contact with few men; they have female-dominated occupations, jobs, and work role sets. This is a small group—thirty-three women—because few women do not work with men. Because of their limited contact with men, other, nonsexual aspects of the female sex role should be emphasized in these jobs. Sexual harassment should not be a problem for them and their work ambience should not be sexualized. Only 21 percent of the women in this group reported being in supervisory positions, but 88 percent said they had a supervisor. Among the women in this group were a bank teller, a keypunch operator, a legal secretary, a telephone operator, a nursing aide, and several preschool and elementary school teachers.

Since the boundaries of the four groups are arbitrary, they will be compared to the total sample of women where appropriate. Some of these results from the total sample appeared in earlier chapters. Here they serve as base rates.

The Men. Only nine men (2.2 percent of the sample of men) were in female-dominated occupations and jobs. Among the nine were a registered nurse, a cashier, a waiter, and an elementary school teacher. Six of the nine men reported that they were in supervisory positions. In contrast, fifty-three men (13.1 percent of the male sample) were in male-dominated occupations and jobs but female-dominated work role sets. Among the men in this group were several managers, a purchasing agent, several engineering technicians, a telephone installer, and a bus driver. Sixty-two percent of these men said they were in supervisory positions;

76 percent said they had supervisors themselves. These two groups of men correspond most closely to the two groups of women expected to experience the most social-sexual behavior at work.

Few men held integrated jobs that correspond to the definition of integrated work used here, that is, integrated occupation and job and opposite-sex dominated work group. Only eight men were in integrated jobs. Among them were two college professors, two real estate agents, and a postal clerk. The comparison group of traditional employees—male-dominated occupation, job, and work group—contained fifty-six men. Most of them had blue-collar jobs, including roofer, photoengraver, truck driver, construction laborer, fireman, janitor, longshoreman, and gardener. Only 7 percent of the fifty-six were in professional or managerial jobs. The total sample of 405 men serves as a measure of base rates for the four subsamples.

Sex Role Spillover in Nontraditional Jobs: Women's Experiences. It is expected that women in male-dominated occupations and jobs are treated differently from their male coworkers and are aware of this different treatment. Thus, they are likely to experience a higher frequency of social-sexual behaviors. Furthermore, because they realize that other (male) work role occupants are not experiencing such treatment, nontraditionally employed women will be aware that these behaviors are directed at them as individual women.

The women in male-dominated work were generally more likely than other women to report sexual overtures in their current jobs (Table 1). For all seven categories in Table 1, more women in nontraditional occupations and jobs reported sexual overtures than did women in general or women in sex-integrated work who also interact mainly with men. For example, 74 percent of the women in nontraditional work said they had received one or more sexual comments intended to be complimentary, compared to 50 percent of women in the total sample. A large discrepancy occurred for reports of being touched sexually at the current job between women in male-dominated occupations and working women in general.

These results may indicate that these nontraditionally em-

Table 1. Women's Experiences of Social-Sexual Behaviors.

Experienced on Current Job	Nontraditional (N = 89)	Traditional 1 (N = 100)	Traditional 2 (N = 33)	Integrated (N = 46)	Total Sample (N = 827)
Complimentary comments	74.2%	57.6%	28.1%	42.2%	50.1%
Complimentary looks, gestures	66.3	63.0	45.5	56.8	51.6
Insulting comments	20.2	12.1	3.0	7.5	12.2
Insulting looks, gestures	13.5	16.0	0.0	5.0	9.1
Sexual touching	31.5	18.0	3.0	12.5	15.3
Required dating	6.7	2.0	0.0	0.0	2.8
Required sex	4.5	4.0	0.0	0.0	1.8

ployed women actually did experience more sex at work than did the average employed woman. However, they may also indicate awareness of such behavior. Thirty-six percent of the women in nontraditional work, compared to 22.8 percent of all women, said that sexual harassment was a problem—either a major or a minor one—where they worked. Nontraditionally employed women were three times more likely than working women in general and traditional 2 women to report it as a major problem (see Table 2).

Nontraditionally employed women also reported that their personal characteristics affect how they are treated by men at work. They were more likely than the total sample to report that physical attractiveness influenced how they were treated by men at work (21.6 percent versus 16 percent for the total sample) and that physical attractiveness was more important than having a good personality with respect to treatment by men.

Sex Role Spillover in Traditional 1 Jobs: Women's Experiences. Women in female-dominated occupations and jobs also experience sex role spillover, although for different reasons than do those in nontraditional work. If they interact frequently with men at work, the sex role spillover is most likely to involve the sexual aspect of the female sex role.

Because sex role and work role overlap for this subset of female workers, the spillover perspective predicts that they should report aspects of sexuality in the job itself, rather than as behaviors directed at them as individual women. This is apparent in reports of the importance of physical attractiveness on the job (Table 2). These traditionally employed women who frequently interact with men are more likely than the total sample to say that physical attractiveness is an important part of their jobs. They were also more likely to report that an attractive woman is likely to be hired for their job, suggesting that attractiveness is part of the work role. In addition, an attractive woman, rather than an attractive man, is more likely to be hired. None of the women in traditional work with male-dominated work role sets said an attractive man would be hired over an attractive woman; 40 percent said an attractive woman would be hired over an attractive man.

Traditional 1 women workers are especially likely to think

Table 2. Sexual Ambience at Work: Women's Experiences.

	Nontraditional (N = 89)	Traditional 1 (N = 100)	Traditional 2 (N = 33)	Integrated (N = 46)	Total Sample (N = 827)
Sexual harassment is a major problem at work	9.0%	5.1%	3.0%	0.0%	2.8%
My physical attractiveness is very important in how men treat me at work	21.6	18.0	6.3	13.2	16.0
Physical attractiveness is more important than a good personality in treatment by men	14.8	10.1	3.2	2.5	9.9
Frequent swearing at work	20.5	13.0	3.1	7.5	13.9
Physical attractiveness is important part of job	18.0	23.2	15.2	10.9	18.4
Attractive women likely to be hired on this job over attractive men	12.4	40.0	33.3	2.6	23.1
Most women here dress to be physically attractive	31.5	35.0	21.2	22.5	31.7
Most men here dress to be physically attractive	9.1	18.8	15.6	13.0	15.1
Frequent sexual talk and joking	28.4	35.4	6.3	28.2	24.2
Organization accepts dating among employees	51.2	58.3	52.2	67.9	60.5

that women workers dress to be sexually attractive. Whereas the women in nontraditional jobs also report that women dress to be physically attractive, I would argue that they do so because they feel they will be treated better by their male colleagues if they are attractive. This situation differs from the perception that being attractive is a requirement of the job, which is the situation of the traditionally employed women in male-dominated role sets, as their reports suggest.

Traditionally employed women with male-dominated work groups were also more likely than the complete sample of nontraditionally employed women to say that sexual comments and jokes were common in their places of work. They were, however, less likely than nontraditional employees to report that they were recipients of complimentary sexual comments (57.6 percent versus 74.2 percent) or recipients of insulting comments (12.1 percent versus 20.2 percent). (See Table 1.)

The incidence of sexual harassment may be underreported among these women. While the treatment accorded to nontraditionally employed women may be noticeably different from the treatment of their male colleagues, the treatment of traditionally employed women is similar for all women (see Taylor and Fiske, 1978, on salience effects). If a behavior happens to everyone, it might not be noticed or might not be labeled as sexual harassment. Farley (1978) gave some examples of women who said they were not harassed when all the female workers received the same treatment from a male boss.

A second reason why sexual harassment might be underreported by these women is related to the finding that traditionally employed women in male work groups report a high incidence of sexual joking. As was noted previously, if people think an initiator is joking, they are less likely to label the behavior as sexual harassment. Thus, traditionally employed women may interpret some encounters as attempts at humor rather than as sexual harassment.

Sex Role Spillover in Traditional 2 Jobs: Women's Experiences. Women in female-dominated occupations, jobs, and work groups come into contact with few men at work, and their reports are very different from the reports of women in the traditional 1 group (with male-dominated work groups). Women who work predominantly with women report substantially fewer sexual incidents than any of the other groups shown in Table 1. None of the thirty-three women, for example, reported experiencing insulting sexual looks or gestures or dating or sexual activity as a requirement of the job. Whereas 18 percent of the women in traditional work with male work role sets reported being sexually touched, only 3 percent of women in traditional 2 work reported being sexually touched by a man. The figures for complimentary comments, looks, and gestures were also substantially lower. No doubt, one of the reasons for the lower rates is the lessened contact with men.

The work environment, however, is also substantially different. Only 3.2 percent of the women reported that physical attractiveness is more important on the job than is having a good personality. Compared to the women doing traditional work but having a male work group, these women were less likely to say that women dress to be attractive (35 percent versus 21.2 percent). They also report substantially less swearing and obscene language. Only 6.3 percent of women with female work groups told about frequent sexual comments and jokes, in contrast to 35.4 percent of traditional 1 women. On all of the measures in Table 1, the rates of this group of women were lowest, indicating the lowest levels of social-sexual experiences, the least sexualized work environments, and the least amount of spillover of the sex object aspect of the female sex role.

Sex Role Spillover in Integrated Jobs: Women's Experiences. The women in integrated work but male-dominated work groups are generally less likely than other women working in male-dominated work groups to report sex at their current jobs (Table 1). None of them said sexual harassment was a major problem at work (Table 2). Male and female sex roles seem to be played down in these work environments. Personal physical attractiveness of women in integrated jobs is not perceived to be as important in men's treatment of them. Nor is physical attractiveness as likely to be an important part of the job, according to the low agreement on items about importance of dressing and being attractive. Finally, in spite of the general absence of a sexualized work environment, women in integrated jobs are most likely to report that their organizations accept dating among employees. Perhaps integrated work environments contain less stereotyped sex role behavior but also exhibit less defensiveness about male-female interaction.

Sex Role Spillover: Men's Experiences. Only 9 of the 405 men were in nontraditional jobs as defined here: female-dominated occupation and job. Although their reports are not meaningful because of the small sample size, they suggest that the work environment is not sexualized but that the men might experience some of the less severe social-sexual behaviors. (See Table 4.)

The reports of the men in integrated jobs (integrated occupations and jobs, female-dominated work groups) likewise lack usefulness because only 2 percent of the men surveyed are in such work situations. Those eight individuals appear to work in nonsexualized environments also.

As Tables 3 and 4 indicate, few men work in integrated or female-dominated jobs. Thus, the only meaningful comparisons are between men with traditional jobs and female work groups and men who work in traditional jobs including male work groups. The men in male-dominated occupations and jobs but female-dominated work groups (traditional 2) interact with fewer women than do the men in male-dominated occupations and jobs but female-dominated work groups (traditional 1), and their answers reflect this difference in contact with women. Over 50 percent of the men with female-dominated work groups reported receiving complimentary comments and complimentary sexual looks and gestures, and 25 percent said they were sexually touched by a woman at work. These figures are fairly similar to the reports of women in traditional work with male-dominated work groups. By contrast, the reports of social-sexual activities by men with male work groups are higher than reports by women in female work groups in six of seven categories (compare Tables 1 and 3, traditional 2 data).

Table 4 shows that the work ambience of men in the two classes of traditional work is consistently similar, in sharp contrast to the reports of women. For example, 34.6 percent of the men in the traditional 1 group reported that swearing is common at

Table 3. Men's Experiences of Social-Sexual Behaviors.

Experienced on Current Job	Nontraditional (N = 9)	Traditional 1 (N = 53)	Traditional 2 (N = 56)	Integrated (N = 8)	Total Sample (N = 405)
Complimentary comments	66.7%	52.8%	32.1%	50.0%	46.0%
Complimentary looks, gestures	55.6	56.6	37.0	25.0	47.3
Insulting comments	33.3	13.2	7.3	37.5	12.6
Insulting looks, gestures	11.1	13.7	10.7	37.5	12.3
Sexual touching	33.3	25.0	7.1	57.1	20.9
Required dating	0.0	0.0	1.8	12.5	2.7
Required sex	0.0	0.0	1.8	0.0	1.0

Table 4. Sexual Ambience at Work: Men's Experiences.

	Nontraditional (N = 9)	Traditional 1 (N = 53)	Traditional 2 (N = 56)	Integrated (N = 8)	Total Sample (N = 405)
Sexual harassment is a major problem at work	0.0%	0.0%	5.5%	0.0%	1.2%
My physical attractiveness is very important in how women treat me at work	11.1	15.4	8.0	0.0	6.4
Physical attractiveness is more important than a good personality in treatment by women	0.0	5.8	5.8	0.0	4.3
Frequent swearing at work	0.0	34.6	30.9	12.5	25.6
Physical attractiveness is important part of job	0.0	15.1	7.1	12.5	11.1
Attractive men likely to be hired on this job over attractive women	22.2	13.2	16.4	0.0	15.3
Most men here dress to be physically attractive	11.1	18.9	25.9	0.0	18.5
Most women here dress to be physically attractive	22.2	39.6	29.1	25.0	34.8
Frequent sexual talk and joking	33.3	34.0	35.7	25.0	30.7
Organization accepts dating among employees	62.5	63.0	69.8	62.5	63.3

work, compared to 30.9 percent of the men in the traditional 2 group.

I contended that traditionally employed women who have male-dominated work groups would work in a sexualized work environment. This assumes men are in a position to shape the work environment to emphasize the aspect of the female sex role that they choose. In general, the data support both the contention and the assumption. That women in traditional work with female work groups work in different, nonsexualized environments suggests that men prefer and are able to emphasize the sexual aspect of the female sex role when they numerically dominate the work environment. That traditionally male work environments, as reported by the men, appear to be somewhat sexualized suggests that a sexualized work environment, in particular one characterized by obscene language and sexual conversation, may be an aspect of the male sex role that men, not women, emphasize.

One final interesting difference in the reports of men and women concerns their responses to the question about the organization's stance toward dating among employees (compare Tables 2 and 4). Across categories, women are less likely than men to report that their organization accepts dating among employees. For example, 51.2 percent of the women working in nontraditional work said that their organization accepts dating, in contrast to 69.8 percent of the men who work in traditional work with male-dominated work groups. These reports should be similar because they concern male-dominated occupations, jobs, and work groups. These differences may reflect less about organizational policy and more about women's and men's perceptions of their own potential gains and losses from dating a coworker, supervisor, or subordinate.

Summary

I argued that the sex ratio at work often leads to sex role spillover, which, in turn, often results in sexual harassment. Sex role spillover, the carryover into the workplace of gender-based expectations about behavior, is a mechanism that can be studied empirically as an underlying factor contributing to sex at work. I also argued that sex ratio at work is one of the factors that cause sex role spillover and that sex ratio can be differentiated into at least three components: sex ratio of the occupation, job, and work group. Along with this, I suggested that awareness (of sexual harasssment) will come from feeling that one is treated differently from others in the same situation, while lack of awareness will be associated with being treated similarly.

When members of one gender numerically dominate one occupation, aspects of the sex role for that gender spill over into the work role for that occupation, especially if the numerically dominant gender also occupies the high-status positions in the work group. The sex role spillover is of two types; its effects depend on whether the person is in the majority or minority sex.

For the person in the minority, there is an incongruence between sex role and work role, because the sex role of the majority gender has spilled over to the work role associated with the occupation. The person of the numerically subordinate gender is essentially a role deviate, and these deviating aspects become salient. Hence, a nontraditionally employed woman is "a woman in a man's job." She is perceived and treated differently. Because her gender is salient to herself as well as to others, she perceives this differential treatment to be discriminatory (in general) and harassment (when the content is sexual). She is aware that she receives differential treatment because she is a woman.

Men are not in this position because so few are in nontraditional work. The nontraditionally employed person may be sufficiently uncomfortable that both sexes prefer to avoid the situation. Women are motivated to persist despite the discomfort because many of the jobs involved are high in status, responsibility, or financial remuneration. Men have little to gain, however, by putting up with being role deviates in "women's work." As Jacobs (1983) noted, the men who do go into women's work tend to leave it.

A second type of sex role spillover is to the job itself. Most workers are treated similarly. In the case of women, this sets up a condition under which they generally will be unaware of sexual harassment. If harassment happens to other workers in the same job, it is viewed as part of the job and therefore acceptable (or at least expected). The sexuality aspect of the female sex role spills over to work role when the occupation is female dominated, the job is female dominated, and the work group is male dominated. Men in traditional work with female work groups do not face the same kind of problems that women do because women do not focus on male sexuality the way men choose to focus on female sexuality. Thus, the traditionally employed man with a female-dominated work group is not expected to be physically attractive and dress to be attractive to women. Women in comparable positions are expected to be attractive and dress to be attractive.The traditionally employed man with a female-dominated work group does, like his female counterpart, experience a variety of less serious social-sexual behaviors.

Sex integrated work shows less sex role spillover and fewer problems with sex at work. Women in integrated work are less likely to have the problem of either traditional or nontraditional women employees. Neither the male nor the female sex role is emphasized in sex integrated work. In this study, few men (about 2 percent) were in sex integrated work.

Research explicitly testing the tenets of the sex role spillover perspective is needed to confirm these tentative results. These preliminary analyses, however, substantiate the general utility of this framework in understanding sex and the workplace.

Implications for Organizations

The plight of the solo or token woman has been described by several social scientists (Kanter, 1977b; Martin and Pettigrew, in press; Northcraft and Martin, 1982; Taylor, Fiske, Etcoff, and Ruderman, 1978). Many difficulties arise just from being one of a kind or numerically rare. For example, the numerically rare woman is especially visible in a group and may feel socially isolated or pressured to perform better than everyone else, but may also feel pressured to conform to others' expectations of her. In addition to the other hurdles she must face, she is also subject to more sexual harassment than other women are. Several observers (Kanter, 1977a; Martin and Pettigrew, in press) have suggested that organizations should try to prevent such solo situations as a lone woman in the shipping department or accounting. Assigning women in pairs or small groups may alleviate some problems they face. Where that is not possible, it is probably a good idea to find an understanding person in the department to offer support. The person could be anyone who appreciates the woman's difficult position and is willing to hear her problems and serve as her ally, someone whom she trusts with issues like sexual harassment. Managers often do not appreciate the extremely difficult and socially isolating position of a solo or token worker. Sexual harassment is only one of many problems such a worker faces.

The dilemma of the numerically rare person has been acknowledged to some degree, if inadequately, but the dilemma of the numerically dominant has not been discussed at all. The issue of harassment arises when women are in all female groups working mainly with men. Cocktail waitresses and flight attendants are two such groups, but there are others that are less visible. Aerospace firms, for example, frequently have clerical groups (all female) and technical groups (almost all male). It is easy for the technical workers and managers to quickly shift from thinking of the clerical staff as clerical workers to thinking of them as women or "girls." Especially young, attractive clerical workers can become targets of overtures from men on the technical staff who assume that the "girls" are there to serve all their whims.

I am familiar with several organizations with this division of labor—male technical staff and female clerical staff—that suffer from high turnover of the clerical staff. The clerical staff regularly complains about unprofessional and rude treatment by the technical staff. It is easy to see how the organization's problem arises. Confounding sex role and work role seems almost natural when jobs are completely sex segregated. Jobs are not going to become sex integrated overnight. In the meantime, management is responsible for trying to prevent the overlap of work role and sex role. Such an effort is a positive step toward preventing complaints of sex discrimination and sexual harassment, lowered morale and commitment to the company, and absenteeism and turnover.

NINE

Common Themes
and Recommendations
for Management

In this chapter, I offer some final observations as well as recommendations for eliminating problematic sex from the workplace. I have divided the chapter into a series of themes that primarily summarize and synthesize findings, interpret findings, and suggest organizational change and plans for action. At the beginning of the book, I stated that sexual harassment is a problem at work but one that is not particularly resistant to change. This chapter concludes with a comprehensive, but inexpensive, plan for eliminating sexual harassment from organizations.

Synthesis

The following themes, which synthesize and summarize material covered earlier in the book, include a consideration of sexual harassment and sexual interest, the sex role spillover concept, and the distinctions between women's and men's work.

Sexual Harassment Versus Sexual Interest. This book has stressed the usefulness of viewing sexuality at work along a continuum from benign or positive expressions of sexual interest to sexual coercion and exploitation (Gutek and others, 1980). This

viewpoint is necessary to understand the frequency and severity
of sexual harassment and the variety of behaviors that people consider sexual. For example, it is difficult to specify a set of behaviors that will always be considered sexual harassment regardless
of the circumstances. People vary dramatically in their responses
to general categories of behavior such as sexual touching. While
84 percent of the surveyed women thought sexual touching was
sexual harassment, 58 percent of the men thought it was sexual
harassment. And when asked about their experience of "being
expected to go out with someone with the understanding that it
would hurt your job situation if you refused or help if you accepted," people described incidents that varied from overt threats
about being fired if they did not comply to normal work-related
business meetings or lunches that happened to involve a person
of the opposite sex.

No doubt some reactions to the phenomenon of sexual harassment rest on the variety of meanings and experiences that
have been included under this label. Presumably the people who
respond to a question about dating as a requirement of the job
with a report about a conventional work-related meeting assume
others are also referring to such behavior when they talk about
dating as a job requirement. My findings and other studies (see
U.S. Merit Systems Protection Board, 1981) show that the most
frequent social-sexual behaviors in the workplace are not severe
sexual harassment. Thus, there may be some justification for articles decrying the fuss over sexual harassment or suggesting that
recipients should feel flattered rather than offended, if the writers
of those articles are thinking about business lunches or comments
meant to be complimentary. It is important, therefore, to distinguish among severe sexual harassment, one-time mild mistreat-
ment of employees, and nonsexual work-related interchanges.

Sex Role Spillover. A major premise of this book is that sex
role spillover is a useful concept to help explain sexuality in the
workplace. Sex role spillover is the carryover of gender-based expectations about behavior from other domains to the workplace.
When women are treated in a manner consistent with the female
sex role while men in the same position are treated in a manner
consistent with the work role, sex role spillover occurs. Because I

am studying sexuality at work, the sexual aspects of male and female roles, especially the sexual object aspect of the female sex role, are of special interest.

The research findings provide abundant evidence for the existence of sex role spillover. Jobs that women hold tend to require physical attractiveness and a pleasant personality, aspects of the female sex role. Both sexes contend that they dress to be attractive to the other sex, but women and men both think that women do this more than men. Some workers acknowledge that they are expected to flirt with the other sex at work or at least feel some pressure to do so. A majority of both sexes report that they have received some kind of social-sexual overture from the opposite sex.

The research shows that employers exhibit some concern about sex role spillover, but view it as a problem of individuals who might not conduct themselves properly. Some organizations disapprove of dating between employees, for example.

Employees may also recognize some of the symptoms of sex role spillover but they, like employers, tend to attribute the evidence not to spillover but rather to individual behavior. Few employees agreed that sex role expectations influence people's behavior at work. Most of them thought that people could prevent sexual overtures if they wanted to, and both sexes tended to think that preventing sexual overtures was equally easy for men and women.

Men's Work and Women's Work. This research project has been able to paint a psychological profile of men's work and women's work and, in the process, document some of the differences between the work experiences of the two sexes. If they have a supervisor, working men almost always have a male supervisor. Many men come into contact with women at work only as subordinates with some other job title, a job title that the man never held and probably does not understand or appreciate. Because men may not understand and appreciate women's jobs, the men may be likely to treat women workers as women, to confound work role and sex role. Because men are more frequently in highly paid and highly prestigious jobs than women, if they treat women "as women," the women are unlikely to complain. Perhaps because men occupy more of the supervisory and powerful positions at work, they can demand and get physically attractive, pleasant, and compliant women in low-level positions if they wish.

Women, on the other hand, almost always have a supervisor in their work. Although the direct supervisor may be female, at some higher level the supervisor is likely to be male. Women usually work with men higher in status if not in a direct supervisory capacity. Thus, women's jobs seem to be more closely supervised and regulated than men's jobs. Because high-status men can demand personal attractiveness from female subordinates, many women are expected to be physically attractive on their jobs, and even more are expected to have "pleasant personalities." These attributes may be more important than their task-specific skills and knowledge.

Perhaps the most outstanding characteristic of both women's and men's work is the relative segregation of each sex from the other. Work is probably a more sex segregating experience than most other areas of activity. Jobs are more sex segregated, for example, than college majors (Jacobs, 1983, 1985). Jobs in any given organization are more sex segregated than occupations across organizations. Furthermore, men's work is more sex segregated than women's work. The greater sex segregation of men is consistent with Lipman-Blumen's (1976) theory of homosociality, which asserts that people prefer their "own kind." She contends that men particularly seek out and prefer being with their own sex. If men are more homosocial than women, it is not surprising that they interact with women at work less than women interact with men.

Sex segregation leads, among other things, to skewed sex ratios, which in turn are related to sex role spillover and a variety of social-sexual activities at work. The relatively rare situation of sexually integrated work appears to be associated with a relaxed atmosphere toward dating but also with less emphasis on male and female sex roles, fewer propositions and overtures, and less harassment.

Sex integration of work is expected to have a variety of favorable consequences for women workers. It generally means access to higher-paying jobs, many but not all of which are high in one or more desirable job characteristics such as status, power, challenge, opportunity for promotion, job security, and fringe benefits. It also means a reduction in social-sexual activity, one more potential benefit of sex integration of jobs for women workers in that social-sexual activity is associated with lower job satisfaction among women. In the area of social-sexual activity, as in such other areas as pay and opportunity for promotion, women stand to gain more from integrating work than men do because social-sexual harassment and interest cause more problems for women than for men.

Is Sexual Harassment a Problem at Work? Sexual harassment has created a stir in the media. Most people in Los Angeles and in other cities of the United States have heard the term and have a general sense of its meaning. Among the many aspects of sexual harassment, they are probably most curious about the magnitude of the problem. How big a problem is it for organizations? How big a problem is it for workers?

Many large organizations have established policies condemning sexual harassment, and many have guidelines instructing victims and managers about proper channels for handling the problem. Collins and Blodgett (1981) found that (male) top management was much less concerned about harassment than (male) middle managers, who were less concerned about it than female workers. Some organizational response to sexual harassment complaints comes, no doubt, from an effort to remove unprofessional and inappropriate conduct from the workplace.

Some organizational response also comes from a fear of being sued. Since sexual harassment has been legally defined and recognized, organizations have become relatively responsive to harassment as a problem. Court cases are costly for organizations not simply because plaintiffs can win large awards but also because organizations pay their own legal staffs well. In addition, a court case has other expenses. The psychological costs in disruption of work, lost hours, and lowered morale also take their toll. Because of the visible effects of lawsuits, organizations, particularly through the eyes of top management, may see sexual harassment primarily as yet another area in which they can be sued and only secondarily as a problem that may reduce the organization's productivity. The costs of law suits and the formal grievance process are much more visible than the costs of lowered commitment and productivity, diminished job satisfaction, and turnover that result from sexual harassment.

For women, sexual harassment may represent a major workplace problem or a minor annoyance. In comparison to such major issues for women workers as adequate daycare, equal pay, or discrimination in hiring and promotion, sexual harassment is a minor problem. Only 3 percent of the women in the sample said it was a major problem where they work, and up to half of all working women have not been harassed on the job. A much larger proportion are probably underpaid relative to their job responsibilities and qualifications. In addition, many of those who have been harassed have resolved the situation in a way that is more or less satisfactory to them. Finding adequate daycare and working for inequitably low wages are problems that go on for years.

On the other hand, for women who have quit or been fired because they were harassed or for women who have put up with a barrage of comments or unwelcome touching, sexual harassment may represent a much greater personal problem than unequal pay or inadequate fringe benefits. All in all, it is difficult to rank sexual harassment in the list of concerns of working women. Trying to do so is probably unproductive. It is a problem worthy of attention both because it does affect a large proportion of women and because it appears to be relatively easy to solve. Unequal pay is a much thornier problem and providing adequate daycare is a much more expensive problem.

Determining how problematic sexual harassment is for working men is much easier. Sexual harassment is not a problem for them. Although men report receiving social and sexual overtures from women, they do not feel harassed. Nor are they harassed the way women are harassed. Most of the overtures they report come from attractive young women who are not married, are either coworkers or subordinates, and who may have been encouraged by the men to make these overtures. The incidents that men report rarely affect their work or their opportunities for advancement. They do not quit jobs or ask for transfers to avoid their harassers. It seems likely that some of the incidents they report would not even be considered sexual by them if the same behavior was initiated by another man or by an older or less attractive woman. For example, when a man suggests discussing a sale over lunch, he probably would not consider this a sexual overture, but when an attractive woman makes the same suggestion, he might.

One indication that sexual harassment is not a problem for men at work is their reluctance to label incidents as harassment. They are more likely than women to consider sexual overtures and comments as appropriate work behavior (Gutek, Morasch, and Cohen, 1983). For men, the less severe types of social-sexual behavior are generally considered appropriate, enjoyable, ego enhancing, or confidence building for them; they may subtly encourage these overtures from attractive young women who work near or for them. When first introduced to the idea of sexual harassment, some men respond, "What's wrong with me? I've never been harassed" (see Collins and Blodgett, 1981). (In the course of this research, about a dozen men and one woman made such a comment to me.)

Finally, the conclusion that sexual harassment is a problem for women but generally not for men can also be inferred from the effects they report. The effects, not surprisingly, are consistent with people's experiences. Women rarely report favorable effects of sexual interchanges. Almost all of their outcomes are negative, ranging from quitting a job to lowered job satisfaction. Furthermore, most of these actions are work related, not personal. Although some women also note that their physical well-being or their relationships with men in general are affected, more often their work life is affected.

Men, on the other hand, rarely report negative effects; some report positive outcomes. Furthermore, these outcomes tend to be personal, not work related. Men's work is virtually unaffected by their social-sexual experiences. When men report positive outcomes, they almost never claim that their work or position at work has improved, but their social-sexual experiences sometimes result in new female friends or dating partners. Some men use work to establish sexual and dating relationships without the attendant risks that women take. Mixing work and sex is rarely a problem for individual men; it often is for women.

Interpretation

Although the following themes also summarize and synthesize findings, they more often go well beyond the narrow confines of the data to consider their meaning. What are the implications of sex and the workplace for women, for men, and for organizations? What are the dynamics involved that allow such a common phenomenon to remain relatively invisible and unstudied for so long?

Pervasiveness of Sexuality. One inescapable conclusion of this project is that sexual behavior in various forms is present in the workplace, even though work organizations do nothing overt to encourage sexual overtures among employees. Few people are likely to contend that one goal of work organizations is to satisfy people's sexual interests or that the workplace should serve that function. Thus, sex at work occurs in an arena generally viewed as inappropriate to the expression of sexuality, which might cause one to ponder whether any sexless environments exist. If the workplace, a setting that symbolizes rationality, efficiency, productivity, and business, engenders so much sex, is it possible to design an environment where gender would be irrelevant and sexual overtures would not be made? Is it possible to create a social setting that actually conveys the message that "sex is inappropriate here"? Probably not. To the ingenious, motivated person any setting can be used to establish a sexual relationship: a funeral home, church, hospital, library, research laboratory. Most of the sex at work, however, does not grow out of a person's interests in establishing a long-term relationship with another employee. Some of it is a display of power, and much of it occurs only because sexuality permeates the work environment. Organizations need not fear they are interfering with love and romance by exerting some influence and control over sexual behavior that is exploitative or hostile. Creating a work environment free of the pervasive influence of sexuality is a task handled better by some organizations than others. Because these workplaces have some advantages over more sexualized environments, they should provide some motivation to make changes. Women, in particular, are more satisfied with their jobs when sexuality in the work environment is minimized. Schneider (1982) suggested that women can exploit their sexuality at work and also be exploited for their sexuality. The findings suggest that the latter occurs more than the former. Yet both sexes tend to think most people are flattered by overtures. Thus, the probability that all employees (or even women employees) will work together to desexualize work environments appears to be very low.

Top managers may be more likely to show interest in reducing the amount of sexuality occurring in some departments of their organizations if they recognize some concrete advantage to doing so. Most executives apparently think that little sexuality exists and whatever does exist is benign in its effects on the organization and on organizational members (Collins and Blodgett, 1981). Cartoons and jokes about executives with attractive and sexually desirable secretaries and assistants (such as Dolly Parton in *Nine to Five*) are legion, but they are rarely critical of the situation.

Recently, some managers are increasingly willing to set up and enforce regulations. Yet regulations alone are not likely to eliminate sexual harassment just as affirmative action regulations alone have not eliminated the problems they set out to solve. As this study showed, work environments characterized by sexual comments and overtures are the same ones that frown on dating among employees, whereas sex integrated environments that have no regulations about employee dating also have relatively little overt expression of sexuality.

What Do Women Want? Freud was supposed to have asked this question. A variation is: Do women like sexual overtures and propositions at work or not? The survey provides a wide range of answers based on different questions. If you believe what women say about women in general, then the answer is "probably most of the time; yes." If you prefer to believe what men have to say about women in general, then the answer is "yes, in most cases." If you prefer to believe what women say about themselves, then the answer is "almost never."

These findings are difficult to interpret and are complicated by a set of cultural attitudes and beliefs about women that
men and women share. According to these beliefs, women are
concerned about their relationships with men above all else, wom-
en's concerns about being attractive to and desired by men over-
whelm their other interests, and women care more about their
appearance than men do. Women and men share these cultural
beliefs and attitudes about women.

Whether or not these beliefs are true in other environments, they are not so at work. In fact, various evidence suggests
we should believe what women say about themselves—that they
do not like sexual overtures, propositions, or comments—more
than we should believe what either men or women say about
women in general. For example, women who experience different
kinds of social-sexual behavior, including sexual comments meant
to be complimentary, are less satisfied with their jobs than other
women are. Women are also more likely than men to label a variety of social-sexual activities sexual harassment.

Individual women seem to realize that being attractive to
men is not their prime motive for working. They do not seem to
realize that other women feel the same. Until they do, they are
not likely to convey the message to men because they think they
are unique in departing from the prevailing attitudes about
women.

Invisibility of Organizational Structure. In general, people in
organizations seem to underestimate the impact of organizational
structure on their behavior. The research on attributions generally contends that people attribute causality to actors rather than
to the characteristics of the environment. Although much of this
research has been done in laboratory situations, the results seem
applicable to sexuality in the workplace. Most workers seem to
think social-sexual behaviors are interpersonal events, unaffected
by the structural characteristics or the climate of the workplace.
For example, female victims were likely to blame the individual
harasser or even occasionally themselves for harassment. Only a
minority reported that the psychological climate was a noticeable
influence. With respect to attitudes about sexuality at work, workers played down the effects of sex role expectations and tended

to report that people who were propositioned encouraged it. Among the open-ended comments were reports of some employees who behaved seductively toward the respondent. The respondent invariably interpreted such behavior as an attempt to gain privileges. No one who reported such seductive behavior suggested that the seductive person was responding to organizational ambience or sex role expectations.

This research suggests that workplaces varied in the extent to which they were sexualized. Yet literally no one compared workplaces in their comments about incidents. That is, no one made a comment such as, "In the last place I worked, there were lots of sexual jokes that the foreman encouraged, but this place is different."

Another aspect of structure that is relatively unnoticed is hierarchy. In the open-ended comments, some women mentioned the actions of supervisors: "I guess it was because he was a supervisor and thought he could get away with it," for example. But rather than blame the hierarchy, they always blamed individuals who were abusing their authority. Likewise, the analyses of attitudes about sexuality showed that both sexes invariably felt both women and men encouraged any overtures they received. Thus, respondents seem to be relatively oblivious to the effects of occupational status, power, and authority as they constrain and limit workers' behavior.

The organizational struture and the social structure may not be a source of blame in all or even the majority of incidents, but employees seem to act as if structure had no effect on their behavior whatsoever.

Micromanipulation Versus Macromanipulation. Lipman-Blumen (1984) made a useful distinction between macromanipulation and micromanipulation that bears directly on the invisibility of organizational structure. Lipman-Blumen contends that "When the dominant group controls the major institutions of a society, it relies on macromanipulation through law, social policy, and military might. . . . The less powerful become adept at micromanipulation, using intelligence, canniness, intuition, interpersonal skill, charm, sexuality, deception, and avoidance to offset the control of the powerful" (1984, p. 8). Macromanipulation is not viewed as manipulation because it is embodied in social institutions; people are unaware of its influence. The emphasis on sexual aspects of the female sex role in male-dominated environments is an indication of macromanipulation by the dominant group of workers.

The situation of traditionally employed women with male-dominated work groups is a particularly good example of this macromanipulation. Women numerically dominate the occupation and the job, thereby facilitating sex role spillover, and men, who apparently wish to emphasize the sexual aspects of the female sex role, dominate the work role set. This macromanipulation is not obvious or transparent to either the dominant male group or the subordinate (either in numbers or power) female group. Because it is embodied in social structure, this manipulation escapes being attributed to the biological or psychological needs or imperatives of the dominant group. The sexualized work environment is not viewed as an outgrowth of male psyche. Instead, it is considered part of the background, taken for granted and unquestioned.

On the other hand, the micromanipulation of women is noticed by both women and men; it is not ignored, and its roots are traced, correctly or incorrectly, to women workers and their biological and psychological makeup. A woman worker's response to an environment that encourages seduction is viewed as an outgrowth of her female psyche. The open-ended comments of workers indicated concern that some women might be willing to trade sexual favors for privileges at work. This is viewed as a form of manipulation by women but might properly be viewed as a response to the macromanipulation of men in power. Micromanipulation is a response to structure, rather than a personal problem of the micromanipulator. The findings from the Los Angeles County survey support this point of view: Women in female-dominated work are in a rather asexual work environment, characterized by very low levels of sexual jokes and comments, sexual overtures, and sexual harassment, and little emphasis on dressing and acting sexually attractive and personable. The suggestion that women "naturally" behave in a sexual or seductive manner is not supported by the findings of this study. They respond in a sexual manner only when such behavior is encouraged or elicited, either specifically by individual men or by a general norm in the workplace.

Trivializing Effect of Sex. One subtle effect of sex in the workplace is to trivialize the work in environments where physical attractiveness is emphasized. Sex can also trivialize a person's accomplishments; some women understand this effect even though they may not verbalize it. When being physically and sexually attractive is an explicit part of a job, people naturally assume the job does not require a lot of other qualifications. Although physical attractiveness and personable behavior are always assets, when a job requires highly specialized skills, it is difficult to imagine that one might also require physical attractiveness and a pleasant personality. Imagine a company recruiting a molecular physicist or a software engineer with the addendum that only the physically attractive and personable need apply.

While a flight attendant, secretary, or receptionist does not have the specialized skills of a molecular physicist or software engineer, these jobs do require specific skills, broad social skills, and motivation, but sociable and physically attractive people are hired. The extent to which the importance of physical attractiveness is emphasized over the job holders' specific skills, motivation, and educational credentials determines how much the job will be devalued and trivialized. The work is viewed as so simple "any pretty young woman will do." When only attractive people are found in a job, others will assume that (1) physical attractiveness is the most important prerequisite of the job and (2) the job does not require other skills or abilities. In this case, the job is trivialized.

Similarly, when an employee is complimented for physical attractiveness or a good personality, a subtle side effect may be to draw attention away from work accomplishments. The character played by Dolly Parton in the movie *Nine to Five* was a good example of this phenomenon. She was an accomplished secretary but everyone believed she held her job because of her physical assets. In this case, her boss actively encouraged that belief, never discussed her work accomplishments, and fostered a rumor of an affair between them. The finding that women frequently view sexual overtures from men as insults may reflect their basic understanding that they make a trade-off between being sexual and being skilled workers. The effect of the sexual compliment is a trivialization of their work. Although few jobs held exclusively or predominantly by men require men to be physically attractive, the same dynamics probably apply.

Sexual Aspects of Male and Female Roles. When social scientists and lay people alike discuss the characteristics of male and female sex roles, they frequently mention that sex object is an aspect of the female sex role. Several women in the survey said they were treated like sex objects or that men expect women to be sex objects. The male role does not seem to immediately evoke a sexual aspect. Men are expected to be initiators in sexual interaction, but that aspect of the male role is much less frequently mentioned than being aggressive, analytical, and rational and exhibiting leadership characteristics. Although men seem to be the more sexually active of the two sexes, their sex role, as it is defined in the United States, does not accord a central place to sexuality. A description of the male sex role, especially as measured in masculinity scales, suggests that men are practically asexual. Nothing could be farther from the truth.

The work environments of men are sexualized, and men work in more sexualized environments than women do. A few writers have discussed the sexual aspects of the male sex role (Gross, 1978; Korda, 1976). The sex role for men includes talking about sex, approaching women as sex objects, and displaying a readiness for sexual interaction. Men maintain the image of sex seekers by making jokes and innuendos. Some of this behavior is for the benefit of the men. Men advertise their heterosexuality by making overtures to women. The spillover of men seeking sex probably accounts for the sexualized environments in male-dominated work.

Women more than men, however, feel the repercussions of sexualized environments. A man apparently can make sexual jokes and comments, use sexual obscenities, proposition women at work, dress to attract women, and still be considered a desirable worker: analytical, rational, tough, a good leader. The sexual aspect of the male sex role does not interfere with the perception of men as serious, professional workers.

A woman cannot be an analytical, rational leader and a sex object at the same time. When she becomes a sex object, her status as a sex object overpowers other aspects of her sex role and completely overwhelms the work role she is trying to occupy. What is doubly troublesome about this dichotomy is that women may not be choosing between the two. A female employee might decide to be a sex object at work, especially if her job is not important to her. More often, however, she chooses not to be a sex object but may be so defined by male colleagues or supervisors anyway, regardless of her own actions.

To avoid being cast in the role of sex object, a woman may have to act completely asexual. Then she is subject to the charge of being a "prude," an "old maid," "old-fashioned," or "frigid," and in her attempt to avoid being a sex object, she is still stereotyped by her sexuality. Men evaluate women in terms of sexuality whether or not women behave in a sexual manner. Kanter (1977a) labeled women who would not conform to any other female stereotype as "the iron maidens"; they have their own share of problems, which Kanter detailed.

However, the main point is that under certain working conditions, a woman may have to present an image of complete asexuality to avoid becoming a sex object and avoid its consequences: being propositioned, "complimented," and harassed while not being considered a serious employee (MacKinnon, 1979). But men can be sexual human beings and productive workers at the same time.

A male-dominated work environment characterizes the dilemma women face. A work environment numerically dominated by men will be characterized by a sexual ambience and the expression of male sexuality. This takes the form of comments about women in general, pictures and posters, sexual jokes and analogies, and obscenities. Although the environment is sexualized, it apparently does not particularly affect the men in it. When a woman enters such an environment, however, she becomes the target of much of the "floating sexuality" already present. She does not usually welcome this attention, although many of the men in that environment probably think she does. Some men may even assert that she picked the job because she welcomes sexual

propositions and comments; they may interpret some of her behavior as sexual when she is merely trying to be friendly (Abbey,
1982; Henley and Mayo, 1981; Henley, 1977). When a woman
does go along with the sexual jokes and comments in an attempt
to be friendly or fit in, she runs the risk of being propositioned
and harassed and, in addition, being viewed as frivolous and unprofessional, not a committed employee.

Using Sex at Work. I have noted in several places in this book
that to the extent people "use" sexuality at work, women are the
ones expected to do so. That stereotype probably developed because women are assumed to be the "carriers" of sexuality, with
sexuality viewed as a resource to be used. Women's presence and
behavior then elicit a sexual response from men. The frequent
comments of men ("she was asking for it") and women ("1 was
wearing red pants") express this point of view. When a woman
wears a tight skirt, a sheer blouse, or no bra or makes a comment
to a man, she is viewed as "using" her sexuality. As carriers of
sexuality, women can use this resource, giving them an unfair
advantage over men who lack the resource, or so some believe.
Some men and women in the survey believed that, by use of this
resource, women do receive organizational rewards they would
not otherwise obtain. When the stereotype is carried to an extreme, it leads people to believe that any woman who has advanced did so by using her sexuality. By implication, she does not
deserve the position she occupies, and people may ostracize her
or treat her with hostility.

This study has found relatively little evidence that women
routinely or even occasionally use their sexuality to try to gain
some organizational goal. There is even less support for the position that women have succeeded or advanced at work by using
their sexuality. Only 1 woman out of over 800 said she used sex
to help her achieve her present position, and she said she was
"thankful" that she did not have to do that anymore. In comparison, many women reported that they were fired or quit after
they got involved with a man at work. This study revealed virtually
no evidence that women either want to or are successful at using
their sexuality at work to gain an unfair advantage over other
workers.

By contrast, men appear to use sexuality more than women do and in diverse ways. A sizable minority of men say they dress in a seductive manner at work; one man said he encouraged overtures from women by unzipping his pants. More frequently, men offer organizational rewards to women in exchange for sex. Some men use sex in a hostile manner—blatant sexual harassment— either to try to intimidate women to have sex with them or to force a woman to quit her nontraditional job. These actions are all rather unusual.

The average working man may tell sexual jokes, use explicit sexual terms to describe work situations, make sexual comments to coworkers, and display sexual posters and pictures. (Sex and sports, some observers claim, are the two major metaphors of business.) Other men, like women, may feign sexual interest to gain some work-related advantage. Instead of trying for a new typewriter, a lighter work load, or better working hours, men may try to extract extra work from women by engendering loyalty in them. A man may use the bonds of affection to ask a woman to work overtime or perform tasks unrelated to work (stop at the cleaners, buy presents, clean his apartment). Since men are not expected to use sex at work, their behavior is hardly ever interpreted as sexual and the work that is done through their use of sex may instead be attributed to their ability as leaders or some other factor.

Action Plans

The preceding chapters all lead to one conclusion: Some changes should be made. How should an organization begin these changes? What factors should be considered? What to consider when initiating these changes is the focus of this section, which emphasizes organizational change that can eliminate sexual harassment.

Implications of Sex Role Spillover. As Nieva and Gutek (1981) pointed out, the way a problem is explained or defined determines the kind of solution that is proposed. If a problem is viewed as stemming from the deficiencies of an individual, then the obvious strategy for change is to make up the individual's deficits or replace that individual with a better-qualified person.

Another angle on the issue of matching problem and solution is to approach the solution first and then see if a sensible model can explain the problem. This approach is useful if the solution called for by the preferred model of the problem is not a feasible solution. For example, I believe that the sociocultural model of sexual harassment described in Chapter One is a reasonable model of the problem of sexual harassment. However, the implications for change presented by this model—essentially to change society—are not easily made operational. I further contend that the sex role spillover perspective is useful because the implications for change are fairly clear and they can be implemented on an organization-by-organization basis. I assume that tackling change in an organization is more manageable than trying to change our society in one fell swoop.

Thus, one way of evaluating a model that serves as a basis for change is the ease with which change can be carried out. That is probably one reason why individual deficit models never go out of vogue. They provide the simplest (if not the most effective) strategy for change. I assert that removing one harasser from an environment in which sexuality is rampant is a simple but not very effective method of eliminating sexual harassment. The victim might feel some satisfaction but will almost certainly pay for that satisfaction in stress and in diminished job opportunities. The harasser may well be unaware that he is a problem, and his replacement may simply take on the same role. This is precisely what happened in one company. The supervisor of a highly sexualized department was released for sexually harassing several subordinates. Within a year, his replacement was also charged with harassment and was found to have "dated" and promoted several female subordinates.

The sex role spillover model is useful in part because it proposes feasible solutions, broader in scope than the solutions proposed by individual deficit models but more constrained and limited than the solutions proposed by sociocultural models (Tangri, Burt, and Johnson, 1982) or sex role or intergroup models (Nieva and Gutek, 1981). In addition, sex role spillover focuses less on power than does the organizational model provided by Tangri, Burt, and Johnson (1982) (discussed in Chapter One) and should thereby be less threatening to power holders (Lipman-Blumen, 1984). I assume that a proposed solution that does not threaten power holders will be accepted and endorsed more readily than one that bluntly calls for a redistribution of power.

The sex role spillover perspective suggests that people need to be aware, first of all, of the confusion of sex roles and work roles in many places of employment. Second, people need to be aware of the negative repercussions, felt primarily by women. Highly educated women already seem to be somewhat aware of how easily sex role carries over to work role and the costs of confusing the two roles. Most other employees do not think sex roles affect employee behavior. Their implicit model of the problem is the individual deficit model described by Nieva and Gutek (1981) and summarized in Chapter One.

Once people learn about the sex role spillover and its negative consequences, they need to change their behavior. In some work environments, that means desexualizing the ambience. How easily this can be accomplished is not clear. Supervisory style can be tremendously influential. Managers who will not tolerate or condone obscene remarks, sexual propositions, and the like can substantially reduce the amount of sexual harassment in the workplace. Can they reward professional conduct, discourage sexualized conduct, and still maintain a friendly, pleasant work environment for the men in the work unit? I believe they can.

This can be done more effectively through role models than through rules and regulations. While popular and research literature have emphasized the importance of successful role models for women, men need role models, too. Successful nonsexist male managers and supervisors could be visible role models if organizations would call attention to and reward their behavior, perhaps by featuring them in company newspapers, asking them to make presentations to others, and promoting them.

Finally, sexual integration of jobs at all levels should eventually reduce the amount of sex role spillover in sexually skewed work units and the amount of sexual harassment. When the structure of occupations and jobs no longer facilitates confusion and overlap between sex roles and work roles, then sexual harassment in its various forms should cease to be a problem.

Deterring Harassers. Understanding why men harass women makes it easier to set up effective programs to combat harassment. The following reasons for harassment must be categorized as speculative interpretations. They reflect the comments of workers and some careful reading between the lines.

Until recently, sex was a "freebie" for the men who chose to cajole, seduce, pressure, or harass women at work into sexual relationships with them. There were no sanctions against men who used work to find willing or unwilling sexual partners. Some harassment appears to be intentionally hostile and is an attempt to intimidate women and force them out of certain jobs. Some harassment is a display of power, of "showing who's boss." In many cases of harassment, the harasser probably does not realize the extent of his effects on the victim and may be completely unaware of the subtle effects of his behavior. Some harassment may be unintentional, a response to a worker who is viewed as an attractive female rather than as a capable worker. And some harassment is a response to an environment that encourages sexual overtures. Thus, information and awareness about the effects on victims may be enough to reduce some harassment. One step in a program to eliminate harassment is providing information to workers through films, memos, and training programs. If harassment is part of the work ambience, information alone is not likely to be sufficient to stop the harassment. Sanctions are likely to be more effective.

If sexual harassment is no longer free, I believe that almost all of it will disappear. If harassment is noted on performance evaluations, if harassers are no longer promoted or do not receive merit increases, and, in severe cases, if the employee is fired, employees will quickly learn that sex is not free for the taking. Most men are not going to risk losing a job, forfeiting a pay increase, or receiving a low performance evaluation just to sexually touch women at work or try to force someone into a sexual relationship. Any information program should also present the sanctions that will be applied to employees who violate the organization's sexual harassment policy.

The rationale for considering sexual harassment in the organization's reward structure is that sexual harassment affects the organization's productivity and job satisfaction of its female workers. Women are currently 43 percent of the labor force and over 50 percent of adult women are employed, so anything that affects female workers also affects American companies and public sector organizations. Women are no longer a small segment of the labor force whose needs and wishes can be ignored without organizations feeling the effects. The welfare of public- and private-sector organizations is linked to the welfare of their female employees as well as the welfare of their male employees. When the productivity and job satisfaction of a large proportion of an organization's employees are affected, the organization is affected.

A Comprehensive Program for Eliminating Sexual Harassment

I have contended earlier that sexual harassment—sex as a problem at work—is relatively easy to remedy, especially in comparison to the elusiveness of many problems (for example, increasing productivity) and the financial cost of others (replacing antiquated equipment). Given that all sex at work has negative consequences for female workers and provides a congenial setting for harassment, attempts at change need not stop at sexual harassment. Organizations might strive to separate work and sex more generally, a goal of preventive medicine. I am not advocating a return to "outlawing" dating, forcing one spouse to quit a job, or other discriminatory policies. I am advocating a professional work environment, where employees are treated in a professional manner.

The most important aspect of any successful change is motivation. Any organization committed to eliminating sexual harassment can do it with relatively few resources directed at two key areas: (1) backing by top management and (2) incorporation of the change (that is, elimination of sexual harassment) into the organization's reward structure.

Motivation must begin at the top. Any effort at change that lacks the support of top management will be substantially less successful than one with such backing. Furthermore, the rest of the organization must know that top management backs the change.

Employees, including middle managers, can quickly differentiate among policies and memos sent out to conform to various regulations, protect the company from lawsuits, provide information, convey a particular image such as concern for workers' welfare, or express a crucial concern of top management. Everyone in the organization must know and believe that top management supports a particular stance.

One of the ways employees can tell if an issue is important to top management is by the treatment accorded to people who pay attention to the issue. What is important to an organization—important to top management—is, or should be, incorporated into the organization's reward structure. For example, if increasing sales is especially important, people who increase sales should be rewarded. While this point seems patently obvious, it is not always followed or even recognized. Organizations sometimes want one result but reward another. If organizations want to eliminate sexual harassment, people who assist in that effort should be rewarded.

These two points—support of top management and incorporation into the reward structure—suggest several concrete steps:

1. Establish a policy on sexual harassment (or review the current policy) and establish a set of procedures to implement the policy.
2. Vigorously pursue allegations of harassment and act on the basis of evidence found in an investigation.
3. Include sexual harassment (and other unprofessional conduct) in performance appraisals and act on those results.
4. Promote professional behavior and professional ambience throughout the organization.

Establish a Policy and Procedures. Many large organizations already have a sexual harassment policy and may have established a set of procedures. These steps provide a mechanism for uncovering and handling sexual harassment, as well as provide substantial protection against lawsuits, provided the steps are in operation. Unfortunately, the scant information available (Dunwoody-Miller and Gutek, 1985) suggests that most employees are not aware of their organization's policies and procedures. Organizations apparently need to improve the dissemination of information. While some seminars, films, and other training programs on sexual harassment specifically are probably useful initially, in the long run, it is probably more efficient and effective to include sexual harassment along with other problems a worker might have and feel reluctant to discuss (for example, an alcoholic supervisor or a severe family illness). Information on sexual harassment should be included in orientation for new employees. Posters, prominently displayed, telling employees where to call or visit if they have been sexually harassed (or have other problems) will be more effective than a lengthy memo sent to everyone, although a memo announcing a new policy and procedures is likely to be useful. A personal statement from the chief executive officer or an endorsement from top management demonstrates support for the policy.

Because some workers and supervisors may not know exactly how the law defines sexual harassment, they should be able to discuss the topic with someone other than their immediate supervisor. Because the immediate supervisor exerts so much control over a person's work life and because supervisors are frequently the harassers, workers who believe they have been harassed need a neutral third party to whom they can speak. Anyone who believes that workers should to go to their immediate supervisor with any complaint or problem is unaware of, or blind to, the effects of organizational structure and the influence of supervisors on people's careers.

Vigorously Pursue Complaints. Pursuing complaints disrupts work. Investigating an allegation without people knowing about it is difficult. And it is embarrassing for all parties. (One reason why women do not report sexual harassment is because they are embarrassed.) It may be tempting to postpone the whole matter and "see if anything develops." Anything short of prompt and vigorous investigation, however, conveys to employees that the organization is not serious about sexual harassment, exposes the organization to legal liability, and encourages victims of harassment to quit or transfer rather than report it.

Someone other than the supervisor should conduct investigations. In cases with which I am familiar, investigators included the members of the company's legal staff, an outside consultant, a personnel specialist, and an ombudsperson. The investigator should thoroughly understand sexual harassment, its psychological and organizational dimensions, as well as its legal definition. The job of investigator also requires the whole range of skills in handling people. Finally, the organization should act on the findings of the investigation. Thus, before they begin, managers should be prepared to follow the recommendations that arise from investigations.

Include Sexual Harassment in Performance Appraisal. An organization that prepares a sexual harassment policy but promotes known harassers into influential positions is not going to convince employees that it wants to eliminate harassment. Yet sexual harassment is rarely considered in the performance review. A university professor once told me that he could not imagine sexual harassment being discussed as part of the promotion decision in academia. It is not surprising that sexual harassment is widespread across college campuses (Benson and Thomson, 1982; Somers, 1982). The performance review need not deal with sexual harassment as a separate category; after all, harassers are only a small percentage of the labor force.

Evaluation of harassment might be more productively and efficiently handled in a category on unprofessional conduct. An organization has a right to expect employees to follow certain standards of conduct, including treating others with respect and dignity and caring for the organization's resources at their disposal. In the case of harassment, the harasser not only fails to treat the victim with respect but also contributes to lower job satisfaction of the victim and affects the victim's career path. The harasser is thereby squandering the organization's human resources and may be squandering the organization's material resources as well if they are used to pursue the harasser's target. Since sexual harassment (and other unprofessional conduct) affects the well-being of employees and the productivity of the organization, the organization serious about eliminating it will create sanctions against harassment in the reward system.

Some people may be considered exceptions to the organization's standard operating procedures. In several court cases I am familiar with, the defendant has been presented as an especially valuable employee for some reason (for example, he has unique skills or valuable contacts). Employees especially valued by an organization may be able to depart from some standard rules and regulations that others must follow. They may be able to set their own schedules or style of dress, for example, or travel more or less often than others. Their eccentricities are tolerated. Yet, there are limits. Organizations are unlikely to put up with theft or embezzlement even from the most valuable person.

Sexual harassment may be a behavior that, while not condoned, has been tolerated from some valuable employees. In several cases, the woman alleging harassment was told by a manager that the harasser was valuable and if she could not handle him, she should find another job. The effects of harassment on organizations and their female work force suggest that it should be tolerated no more than theft is tolerated. In its effects, sexual harassment is not comparable to personal whims or eccentricities; it is more like embezzlement.

Promote Professional Behavior and Ambience. Promoting professional behavior is a nebulous task but one that makes the workplace pleasant and productive for everyone and prevents a variety of problems from developing. Talented, motivated people prefer to work in a professional environment. Professionalism is not established by fiat but is developed through example and reinforcement. Professionalism should be stressed at orientation for new employees, and appropriate styles of address should be discussed ("honey," "doll," and "sweetie" are not appropriate forms of address for coworkers, for example). Managers at all levels should be role models of professional conduct. Company newsletters, posters, and the like can include small notes reminding people to treat others with respect and courtesy. Professionalism should be considered in the performance appraisal process.

Professionalism carries different connotations to different people. To separate work and sex, the organization must see that people include sexual harassment, unwanted sexual comments, and "girlie posters" in the category of unprofessional conduct. Some may need a reminder of what is unprofessional behavior.

The person who is always attired in a three-piece suit may pinch members of the clerical staff; the person who will "stand by the quality" of his work may cover his work area with pictures of nude women.

Professionalism should not be confused with authoritarianism. The workplace can be professional and informal, with a maximum of individual discretion involved. A professional ambience may prevent some individuals from doing what they want, if what they want is to violate the personal rights of others. If an employee uses racial or sexual slurs in discussing a colleague, we generally consider that unprofessional conduct. Discouraging such slurs allows the potential victims the freedom to work in a nonthreatening environment.

In summary, the goals of eliminating sexual harassment and separating sex and work are in the best interests of organizations and their female work forces. In the short run, disseminating information about a well-conceived policy and set of procedures and putting them into action are important steps in encouraging professional behavior from all employees. These goals are best achieved in the long run by incorporating them into the ongoing practices of the organization: orientation for new employees, messages in the company's newsletter or newspaper, inclusion in the performance appraisal system, and ample role models of professional behavior from the chief executive officer on down.

Sexual harassment was discovered a decade ago. Now in the mid 1980s in the midst of increasingly strong laws and regulations, we are beginning to understand the phenomenon of sex at work, and we know that it has both visible and subtle but pervasive effects with negative consequences. With this new understanding of sex at work and some judicious action plans, I believe it is possible by the mid 1990s to eliminate sexual harassment, leaving a more productive and professional workplace for everyone.

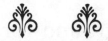

Appendixes:
Research on Sex
and the Workplace

A. Background for the Study
B. Sampling Strategy
C. Main Questionnaire

A: Background for the Study

Most research in organizational behavior is conducted in one or a few organizations. I could have sought permission from several organizations to carry out such a study, but I thought the problem of access would be difficult; when later I tried to find organizations willing to participate in such research, my worst fears were confirmed. Organizations do not want to learn that sexual harassment or any form of sexuality is occurring at work. Even when I did find a supportive manager, the legal department killed the study, arguing that such information would provide ammunition for any employee suing the organization for sexual harassment.

Access is not the only problem with an organizational study. Such a study would lack generalizability; it would represent a poor vehicle for providing base rates on incidence. Further, if a study of one organization did find a high incidence of harassment, other organizations would deny any similarity to the offender and ignore findings or recommendations arising from the study.

I decided that an interview with a diverse group, preferably a representative sample, of working people would be a suitable method of collecting data. Personal interviews in people's homes immediately came to mind. Such interviews are, however, costly and to interview workers, the interviews would have to be scheduled for evenings and weekends. Many interviewers do not like to visit certain areas in the evening. All in all, personal interviews in people's homes did not appear promising.

Nor did mailed surveys, for sexuality at work is an unusual topic, and I had heard that some early mail questionnaires on sexual harassment had resulted in both a low response rate and a high proportion of bizarre answer patterns, suggesting that not everyone answered truthfully or took the questionnaire seriously. The low response rate associated with mail questionnaires—50 percent is considered high (Babbie, 1973)—also meant it was a poor method for gathering base rates on incidence.

Telephone surveys appeared more promising. Telephone interviews are about half the cost of personal interviews and response rates are almost as high. Our experience asking people about personal and financial problems showed that telephone interviews resulted in information comparable to information obtained from personal interviews (Quinn, Gutek, and Walsh, 1980). These findings were consistent with the findings of a large-scale study comparing the two methods (Groves and Kahn, 1979). People may be even more willing to talk about sensitive topics over the phone than they are face to face (Quinn, Gutek, and Walsh, 1980; Groves and Kahn, 1979). To verify my convictions about telephone interviewing, I conducted a large preliminary study on sexual harassment using students as telephone interviewers (Gutek and others, 1980). I also examined the patterns of responses to same-sex versus opposite-sex interviewers (Handschumacher and Gutek, 1980) and found that people responded similarly to them.

Thus a representative survey of working men and women in Los Angeles County, interviewed by telephone in their homes, was selected as the method of study. As one of the geographically largest counties in the United States, Los Angeles County provides a large, diverse sample of mostly urban workers. (The county extends across the San Gabriel Mountains and includes small desert communities.)

The Field Research Corporation of San Francisco was awarded a subcontract to conduct telephone interviews with 800 adult working women and 400 adult working men, randomly selected by random-digit dialing. All working people living in households with telephones in Los Angeles County were eligible for inclusion in the sample. The sampling procedure is described in detail in Appendix B.

Interviews were conducted in English and in Spanish. Women were oversampled because most of the reports of sexual harassment concern female victims. Women also have been most vocal about the negative effects of sex at work. The final sample consisted of 827 women and 405 men, all of whom were eighteen or older, employed outside the home twenty hours a week or more, and regularly came into contact with members of the opposite sex at work as coworkers, supervisors, customers, or clients.

Appendix C contains the interview schedule, which has six major sections. The first section ascertains information about the respondent's job, including job satisfaction, questions about supervision, policies of the organization that affect male-female interaction, amount of contact with the opposite sex, and the importance of physical attractiveness and a good personality on the job.

The second main section assessed the frequency of social-sexual behavior on the current job and on any previous job. This pattern of data collection allowed for an analysis of factors in the work environment that affect social-sexual behavior on the current job, as well as an assessment of the total amount of social-sexual behavior and sexual harassment in the respondent's working life.

Based on the results of two pilot studies (see Gutek and others, 1980), eight types of social-sexual behavior were studied: sexual comments intended to be complimentary, sexual comments intended to be insulting, sexual looks and gestures meant to be complimentary, sexual looks and gestures meant to be insulting, nonsexual touching, sexual touching, dating as a requirement of the job, and sexual relations as a requirement of the job. These categories represent a range of social-sexual behaviors, including some most likely to be called sexual harassment and others unlikely to be called sexual harassment.

The third section of the questionnaire gathered additional information about the more serious forms of social-sexual behavior: sexual touching, dating as a job requirement, and sexual relations as a requirement of the job. The questions concern the individual's assessment of responsibility for a social-sexual incident and the characteristics of the initiating person. This section included open-ended questions about the incident.

The interview's fourth section ascertained respondents' attitudes about the occurrence of sexuality at work, for example, why it happened, how the recipient responded, how the recipient felt, and whether it could be controlled. This section contains twelve questions, and the interviews started at a random point in the twelve questions to minimize the effects of fatigue. Several questions asked about the extent to which workers dress to be attractive or seductive.

The fifth part of the questionnaire concerned respondents' definitions of sexual harassment, the first place in the interview that the term was used. Respondents were asked whether or not each of the eight types of social-sexual behavior mentioned earlier in the questionnaire constituted sexual harassment. This section also assessed negative consequences of sexual harassment such as quitting a job or being fired.

The last section of the questionnaire determined demographic characteristics of the respondent, including age, marital status, education level, family income, spouse's occupational status, number of children, and ethnicity. There were also some questions about the degree of comfort or discomfort felt by the respondent. Finally, the respondent was asked whether he or she would consent to being called back later and asked additional questions.

Some of the respondents were called again as part of a dissertation by Jensen (1981). The 293 women who reported more serious forms of social-sexual behavior—sexual touching and dating or sexual relations as a job requirement—were called again fourteen to sixteen months after the initial contact. The sampling procedures are described in Appendix B and in Jensen (1981), and the questionnaire used is available in Jensen. Major findings of her study of attributions made by victims of sexual harassment are available (Jensen, 1981; Jensen and Gutek, 1982). Chapter Four contains other findings from that study.

The follow-up questionnaire contained questions about the initial incident experienced by the respondent, how she responded to it, how she felt about it, whom she blamed for the incident, whether she reported it to someone, and, if not, why not. The questionnaire also contained information about patterns of interaction with the initiator and included a previously developed measure of sex role attitudes (Smith, Ferree, and Miller, 1975).

The interviewers' questionnaire used in the main study was developed in two pilot studies (described in Gutek, 1982). The first pilot study of 399 Los Angeles County working women and men was carried out in the fall of 1978 (described in Gutek and others, 1980); the second pilot study, with a sample of 281 men and women, was conducted in February 1980.

In addition, the questionnaire prepared for the main study was pretested by the Field Research Corporation interviewing staff. Interviews were conducted over six weeks in the summer of 1980. The follow-up questionnaire was developed in 1981; trained student interviewers, supervised by Jensen, did the interviewing in the fall of 1981.

B: Sampling Strategy

A sampling strategy was devised by the Field Research Corporation, San Francisco, to yield a representative sample of working adults in Los Angeles County stratified by sex. The method of random-digit dialing was used.

The survey universe was defined as persons who fit all of these qualifications: eighteen or older, employed outside the home twenty hours or more a week, and in contact with members of the opposite sex at work as coworkers, supervisors, customers, or clients.

The sample of households to be called was developed by a Field Research Corporation computer program, which generated random four-digit numbers coupled with all prefixes (central office codes) operating in Los Angeles County. In this way, all communities in Los Angeles County fell into the sample in proportion to the population of households with telephones. All operating telephone numbers had an equal probability of being included in the sample, regardless of whether or not they were published in the latest telephone directories.

The Field Research Corporation telephone sampling program produces call record sheets, each of which is a cluster of 20 telephone numbers. For this survey, 490 clusters of 20 listings each were used, or a total of 9,800 telephone numbers from eleven different Los Angeles County telephone directories.

When a person answered the phone, interviewers followed systematic selection procedures to determine the number of eligible persons in the household, if any, and to select that person who was to be the "designated respondent." The research design called for interviews with twice as many women as men. Inter-

185

viewers began by completing interviews with a randomly selected eligible adult in each household, regardless of sex. Once the quota of 400 interviews with men was met, interviewers concentrated on eligible women.

Strictly speaking, the "probability of selection" is not known in advance when one is screening to locate qualified respondents within households, since the incidence of such qualification is not known. In each household, interviewers asked for the first names (or initials) of all eligible adults and listed these in descending order of age on a screening form. A random-selection pattern on the screening form designated the person in the household to be interviewed. The random-selection pattern is often called "the Kish method" (Kish, 1965).

Because the number of eligible respondents varies from household to household and only one interview was to be conducted in each household, the number of eligible respondents in the household determined their selection probability. Then, a post-interview weight, the reciprocal of the number of eligible respondents in the household, was applied to the questionnaire data for each respondent.

In this particular study, independent samples of men and women were sought. However, administrative simplicity and efficiency were gained by assuming independence of male and female selection in the first part of the sampling and interviewing process when interviewers were working to complete the male quota of 400 interviews. This assumption is based on the principle that any given household could be drawn into both the male and female sample frames and that both an eligible woman and man would then be interviewed. However, the chances of a given household falling into both samples are so remote that the bias is virtually zero. Thus, those interviews in households where an eligible man was selected were weighted by the number of eligible men in the household. And those interviews selecting an eligible woman were weighted by the number of eligible women in the household. By following this procedure, comparability was achieved across the two sampling phases.

Interviewers made a minimum of four attempts to reach a spokesperson at a residential household. Businesses and discon-

Table 1. Disposition of Telephone Listings.

	Number
Total telephone listings called	9,800
Unusable listings	4,263
Not assigned, disconnected	2,634
Business listing	1,629
Usable listings	5,537
No answer after all attempts	1,061
Busy on last several attempts	22
No adult available after all attempts	94
Designated respondent not available	198
Communications barrier	75
Terminated after starting (conversion unsuccessful)	30
Declined to cooperate	384
No qualified respondent in household (no one working)	2,221
Selected respondent not qualified	
(does not work with men/women)	160
Other	60
Interviews completed	1,232
Males	405
In English	380
In Spanish	25
Females	827
In English	787
In Spanish	40

Note: Table prepared by the Field Research Corporation, San Francisco.

tinued numbers received no callbacks, of course. Up to two more attempts were made to reach the designated respondent once that person had been identified. If the designated respondent refused or broke off the interview, up to four additional attempts were made to convert that refusal or termination into a completed interview. Callback attempts were made on different days and at different hours during the interviewing period.

Table 1 shows the results of the sampling procedure. The final sample of 1,232 respondents was obtained from 5,537 usable listings. The rejection rate was 23 percent.

To obtain a representative sample of respondents, each case had to be weighted by the number of eligible respondents in the household. A disadvantage of such weighting is that it artificially inflates sample size. Since statistical significance depends, in part, on sample size, the weighted data must be proportionally reduced to the original sample size before one can report statistical significance.

In this data set, the weighted and unweighted distribution of all variables was compared, and I found that all of the distributions of the unweighted variables were within the 95 percent confidence interval of the distribution of the weighted variables. Relatively few households contained more than one eligible man or more than one eligible woman. Thus, the unweighted sample constitutes a generalizable sample of working women and men in Los Angeles County. The profile of the workers in the sample is shown in Table 2. All of the analyses reported here are based on the unweighted data.

Jensen (1981) conducted the follow-up study; the subject pool consisted of 293 women who, in the initial survey, agreed to be recontacted and who reported having experienced one or more of the following social-sexual behaviors either in their present job or in a previous job:

1. Touched in a sexual way by a man on the job
2. Expected to go out with a man at work with the understanding that it would hurt her job if she refused or help her if she accepted
3. Expected to engage in sexual relations with a man at work with the understanding that it would hurt her job if she refused or help her if she accepted.

The follow-up interviews were also conducted by phone. (Only the respondents' phone numbers and first names or initials were known to the researchers.) The telephone interviews were conducted on the Computer-Assisted Telephone Interviewing (CATI) system, developed at the University of California at Los Angeles (see Shure and Meeker, 1978). In using CATI, researchers program the interview protocol into the system; interviewers sit at terminals and enter responses directly into the computer.

The follow-up interview was conducted, on the average, fifteen months after the original interview. On the basis of previous experience with follow-up interviews conducted over a year

Table 2. Characteristics of Random Sample of Working Men and Women.

	Males	Females	
Age	$x = 46.0$	$x = 41.85$	$t = 13.89^a$
Education	$(N = 405)$	$(N = 826)$	$\chi^2 = 17.05^b$
0–8 years	7.4%	3.8%	
9–11 years	4.7	5.7	
12 years	20.7	28.5	
Some college	35.3	35.6	
Bachelor's degree	18.3	16.0	
Graduate school or degree	13.6	10.4	
Marital status	$(N = 405)$	$(N = 825)$	$\chi^2 = 47.20^a$
Married	67.7%	49.9%	
Widowed	1.0	4.6	
Divorced	7.2	15.8	
Separated	2.0	3.9	
Never married	20.0	21.8	
Living together	2.2	4.0	
Spouse's employment	$(N = 283)$	$(N = 445)$	$\chi^2 = 236.30^a$
Full- or part-time	37.8%	90.1%	
Unemployed, looking	2.5	2.2	
Unemployed, not looking	17.0	1.8	
Retired, housewives	42.8	5.8	
No live-in partner	(30.1% of total)	(46.1% of total)	
Have children	$(N = 405)$	$(N = 827)$	$\chi^2 = 22.35^a$
Yes	52.8%	38.5%	
No	47.2	61.5	
Total family income	$(N = 391)$	$(N = 778)$	$\chi^2 = 22.59^a$
Under $10,000	7.4%	12.9%	
$10–19,999	22.8	31.5	
$20–29,999	30.2	23.7	
$30,000 +	39.6	32.0	
Ethnicity	$(N = 400)$	$(N = 824)$	$\chi^2 = 2.58$
White	69.5%	66.4%	
Black	12.3	12.3	
Asian	4.3	4.9	
Hispanic	13.5	15.3	
Other	0.5	1.2	

$^a p < .001.$ $^b p < .01.$

after the original interview, a response rate of 40 percent to fifty percent was expected.

After lists of the 293 eligible respondents were generated, including their identification numbers, first names or initials, phone numbers, and type of incident experienced, trained student interviewers called respondents during weekday evenings and on weekends. Of the 293 eligible respondents, 135 were interviewed again; the response rate was 46 percent. Details of the procedures used in the follow-up study are in Jensen (1981).

C. Main Questionnaire

(Women's Version)

1. Do you ever come in contact with men at work, as coworkers, supervisors, customers, or clients? (If No, interview is terminated.)   Yes   No

2. What kind of work do you do? (What is your job title? What type of industry or service do you work in?)

3. How satisfied are you with your current job? Would you say you are:

   Very satisfied
   Somewhat satisfied
   Somewhat dissatisfied
   Very dissatisfied

4. Do you have a supervisor you report to?

   Yes (Ask question 5)
   No (Skip to question 9)

   (If yes to question 4:)

5. Is your immediate supervisor a man or a woman?

   Man
   Woman

6. Approximately how old is your supervisor? (Just your best guess)

7. How many other employees report to your supervisor?

   1
   2–5
   6–10
   11 or more
   Don't know
   None

8. In general, would you say that your supervisor has a lot of control over what you do at work, some control over what you do, or very little control over what you do?

   A lot
   Some
   Very little

9. How does your organization feel about employees dating each other? Is dating between employees discouraged, tolerated, or accepted?

   Discouraged
   Tolerated
   Accepted

10. Would you say that joking or talking about sexual matters at your workplace happens frequently, sometimes, or not at all?

    Frequently
    Sometimes
    Not at all

191

11. Would you say that workers swear or use rough lan-   Frequently
    guage at work frequently, sometimes, or not at all?   Sometimes
                                                          Not at all

12. Where you work, how much social pressure is there   A lot
    for *women* to flirt with men? A lot, some, or none? Some
                                                          No, none

13. Where you work, how much social pressure is there   A lot
    for *men* to flirt with women? A lot, some, or none? Some
                                                          No, none

14. Thinking just about your job classification at work, More men
    are there more men, more women, or about an   More women
    equal number of each?   Equal number
                                                          No other people in my
                                                             class

15. Would it be harder for men, or harder for women,   Harder for men
    to get this kind of job, or wouldn't there be any   Harder for women
    difference?   No difference

16. Within your organization, is your job high, medium, High
    or low in prestige?   Medium
                                                          Low

17. There are a number of things that may influence   Very important
    whether or not someone is hired or kept in a po-   Somewhat important
    sition. These things may or may not be given in a   Not at all important
    job description. One of these is physical attractive-
    ness. On your job how important is it for *you* to be
    physically attractive? Would you say it is:

18. Who would be more likely to be hired in your job—   Man
    an attractive man, an attractive woman, or wouldn't Woman
    there be any difference?   No difference

19. At your workplace, how important is a woman's   Very important
    physical attractiveness in the way men treat her?   Somewhat important
    Would you say: Not at all important

20. At your workplace, how important is a woman's   Very important
    personality in the way men treat her? Would you   Somewhat important
    say: Not at all important

21. At your workplace, which would you say is more   Physical Attractiveness
    important in the way men treat a woman—her   Personality
    physical attractiveness or her personality?   No difference

22. Do you directly supervise the work of others?   Yes (Ask question 23)
                                                         No (Go to question 24)

(If yes to question 22:)

23. How many people do you supervise?

24. Next are some questions about your contact with   A great deal
    men on your job. First, how much opportunity is   Some
    there for job-related talk with men? Would you say: None

25. How much opportunity is there to talk socially with   A great deal
    men? Would you say: Some
      None

26. How much of the time does your job require that   A great deal
    you work with men? Would you say: Some
      None

27. In general, if you were asked by a man at work to   Flattered
    engage in sexual activity, would you feel flattered   Insulted
    or insulted?   It depends
      Neither, it wouldn't
         happen

28. How often do people treat you disrespectfully at   Very often
    work? Would you say very often, sometimes, rarely,   Sometimes
    or never?   Rarely
      Never

29. How often are you expected to do activities which   Very often
    are not formally a part of your job, such as shop-   Sometimes
    ping for another worker? Would you say very often,   Rarely
    sometimes, rarely, or never?   Never

30. Do men consider your physical attractiveness above   Yes
    average?   No

31. Do men consider your personality above average?   Average/no, not above
    If yes: Would you say well above average or some-   average
    what above average?   Well above average
      Somewhat above
         average

There are various ways a man can behave toward a woman at work in a non-professional way. We think this is a very important part of people's working conditions, and I would like to ask you some questions about it. If any question should make you too uncomfortable, please feel free to say you prefer not to answer it.

32. Sometimes on the job, men make comments of a   Yes
    sexual nature that are meant to be compliments. On   No
    your *present* job, have you ever received sexual re-   Decline to answer
    marks from a man that he meant to be
    complimentary?

33. On any *previous* job, have you ever received sexual   Yes
    remarks from a man that he meant to be   No
    complimentary?   Decline to answer
      No previous job

34. Sometimes on the job, men make sexual comments that are meant to be an insult or a "put-down." On your *present* job, have you ever received sexual comments from a man that he meant to be insulting?

Yes
No
Decline to answer

35. On any *previous* job, have you ever received sexual comments from a man that he meant to be insulting?

Yes
No
Decline to answer
No previous job

36. Sometimes on the job, though they don't say anything, men make looks or gestures of a sexual nature that are meant to be a compliment. On your *present* job, have you ever received sexual looks or gestures from a man that he meant to be complimentary?

Yes
No
Decline to answer

37. On any *previous* job, have you ever received sexual looks or gestures from a man that he meant to be complimentary?

Yes
No
Decline to answer
No previous job

38. Sometimes on the job, even though they don't say anything, men make looks or gestures of a sexual nature that are meant to be an insult or a "put-down." On your *present* job, have you ever received sexual looks or gestures from a man that he meant to be insulting?

Yes
No
Decline to answer

39. On any *previous* job, have you ever received sexual looks or gestures from a man that he meant to be insulting?

Yes
No
Decline to answer
No previous job

40. Sometimes on the job, a man might touch a woman in a way that is *not* meant to be sexual. On your *present* job, have you ever been touched by a man in a nonsexual way?

Yes
No
Decline to answer

41. On any *previous* job, have you ever been touched by a man in a nonsexual way?

Yes
No
Decline to answer
No previous job

42. Sometimes on the job, a man might touch a woman in a way that *is* meant to be sexual. On your *present* job, have you ever been touched by a man in a sexual way?

Yes
No
Decline to answer

43. On any *previous* job, have you ever been touched by a man in a sexual way?

Yes
No
Decline to answer
No previous job

44. Sometimes on the job, a man expects a woman to   Yes
    go out with him with the understanding that it   No
    would hurt her job situation if she refused or would   Decline to answer
    help if she accepted. On your *present* job, have you
    ever been asked by a man to go out with him as
    part of your job?

45. On any *previous* job, have you ever been asked by a   Yes
    man to go out with him as a part of your job?   No
                                                     Decline to answer
                                                     No previous job

46. Sometimes a woman is expected to engage in sexual   Yes
    relations with a man with the understanding that it   No
    would hurt her job situation if she refused or help   Decline to answer
    if she accepted. On your *present* job, have you ever
    been asked by a man to engage in sexual relations
    as part of your job?

47. On any *previous* job, have you ever been asked by a   Yes
    man to engage in sexual relations as a part of your   No
    job?   Decline to answer
                                                           No previous job

(If yes to question 47:)

48. Overall, how responsible would you say you   Very responsible
    were for this happening? Would you say you   Somewhat responsible
    were very responsible, somewhat responsible,   Just a little responsible
    just a little responsible, or not at all responsible?   Not at all responsible
                                                             Decline to answer

(Interviewer: determine which one of the following experiences questions 49–58
refer to. Circle number below:)

(Q.46)   1   being asked by a man to engage in sexual relations as part of your
             present job

(Q.44)   2   being asked by a man to go out with him as part of your present
             job

(Q.42)   3   being touched by a man in a sexual way on your present job

(Q.47)   4   being asked by a man to engage in sexual relations as part of a
             previous job

(Q.45)   5   being asked by a man to go out with him as part of a previous
             job

(Q.43)   6   being touched by a man in a sexual way on a previous job

         7   No incidents reported. (Skip to question 59.)

Now I'd like to ask you about (insert description here):

49. How frequently has this happened to you? Would   Only once
    you say only once, a few times, or many times?   A few times
                                                      Many times
                                                      Decline to answer

(If "a few times" or "many times," say:) Please think about only one experience—
the one you remember most clearly.

50a. Why do you think this happened? _____

_____

50b. What more can you say? _____

_____

51. Overall, how responsible would you say you were   Very responsible
    for this happening? Would you say you were very   Somewhat responsible
    responsible, somewhat responsible, just a little re- Just a little responsible
    sponsible, not at all responsible?   Not at all responsible
                                                       Decline to answer

Now, thinking about the person involved:

52. At the time of the experience, how long had you   Less than 1 day
    worked for or been associated with the man?   1 day to 2 months
                                                       2–6 months
                                                       Over 6 months

53. After the experience, would you say that you got   Better
    along better, the same, or worse with the man than Same
    before the experience?   Worse

54. Is the man your supervisor or one of your   Yes
    supervisors?   No
                                                  Not applicable, have no
                                                    supervisor

55. To your knowledge, has this man behaved in the   Yes
    same way toward other women at work?   No
                                                      Don't know

56. What is his age? Just your best guess.   15–29
                                              30–39
                                              40–49
                                              50–59
                                              60 or older

57. Is he married or unmarried?   Married
                                   Unmarried
                                   Don't know

58. Do women consider him above average in physical   Yes
    attractiveness?   No

(Interviewer, ask everyone:)

59. Next, I'm going to read you a list of statements and would like to know, for

each one, whether you *disagree strongly, disagree somewhat, agree somewhat,* or *agree strongly* with each one. Here's the first one.

a. Sex roles in our society encourage women to request sexual relations from men at work.

b. Many women would see it as complimentary if men at work asked them to have sexual relations.

c. When a woman is asked by a man at work to engage in sexual relations, it's usually because she did something to bring it about.

d. Women who are asked by men at work to engage in sexual relations could have done something to prevent it.

e. Women who ask men at work to have sexual relations with them want to dominate men.

f. Although they may or may not admit it, most women are flattered if an attractive man at work asks them to have sexual relations.

g. Sex roles in our society encourage men to request sexual relations from women at work.

h. Many men would see it as complimentary if women at work asked them to have sexual relations.

i. When a man is asked by women at work to engage in sexual relations, it's usually because he did something to bring it about.

j. Men who are asked by women at work to engage in sexual relations could have done something to prevent it.

k. Men who ask women at work to have sexual relations with them want to dominate women.

l. Although they may or may not admit it, most men are flattered if an attractive woman at work asks them to have sexual relations.

Now I'd like to ask your opinion about a few more things:

60. How many women dress to appear sexually attrac- Most
tive to men at work? Would you say most, some, or Some
hardly any women do this? Hardly any
None

61. How many men dress to appear sexually attractive Most
to women at work? Would you say most, some, or Some
hardly any men do this? Hardly any
None

62. How many women present themselves in sexually Most
seductive ways to men at work? Would you say Some
most, some, or hardly any women do this? Hardly any
None

63. How many men present themselves in sexually se- Most
ductive ways to women at work? Would you say Some
most, some, or hardly any men do this? Hardly any
None

64. Are you familiar with the term "sexual   Yes
    harassment"?   No

65. Well, recently there has been some interest in what has been called *sexual harassment* at work. This usually refers to harassment of women by male workers, clients, or customers, but may also include female harassment of male workers.

    We'd like to find out just what the term *sexual harassment* means to you. Going back to the questions I asked earlier, I want your opinion of whether or not you consider each type of incident we mentioned as **sexual harassment**. For each one I read, please tell me whether *yes, you do consider it sexual harassment; no, you do not;* or *you don't know or aren't sure.* Here's the first one:

    a. Being asked to have sexual relations with the understanding that it would hurt your job situation if you refused or help if you accepted?

    b. Being asked to go out with someone with the understanding that it would hurt your job situation if you refused or help if you accepted?

    c. Touching at work that was meant to be sexual?

    d. Touching at work that was *not* meant to be sexual?

    e. Looks or gestures of a sexual nature that were meant to be insulting?

    f. Looks or gestures of a sexual nature that were meant to be complimentary?

    g. Comments of a sexual nature that were meant to be insulting?

66. How much of a problem at your place of work do   A major problem
    you consider sexual harassment to be? Would you   A minor problem
    say it is: No problem

67. Have you ever quit a job because you were sexually   Yes
    harassed?   No
                                                          Decline to answer

68. Did you ever try to get a transfer or get another   Yes
    job within your organization because you were sex-   No
    ually harassed?   Decline to answer

69. Has being sexually harassed ever upset you enough   Yes
    to talk to a coworker, friend, or someone else about No
    the experience?   Decline to answer

70. Did you ever go after a job but give up on it because Yes
    you thought that you would be sexually harassed?   No
                                                          Decline to answer

71. Do you feel that you have ever been refused a job   Yes
    because you did not respond to sexual requests or   No
    demands?   Decline to answer

72. Have you ever experienced sexual harassment in   Yes
    other places than at work?   No
                                                          Decline to answer

Finally, we'd like to get some general information about you for statistical purposes only:

73. What was the highest grade of school or college you completed?

No formal schooling
1–8 years
9–11 years
12 years/high school graduate
Some college, business, or technical school
4 year college graduate
Graduate degree or more

74. In what year were you born? _____

75. What is your marital status? Are you married and living with your spouse, widowed, divorced, separated, never married, or living together with someone?

Married, living with spouse (Ask question 76)
Widowed (Skip to question 78)
Divorced (Skip to question 78)
Separated (Skip to question 78)
Never married (Skip to question 78)
Living together (Ask question 76)

76. What is your spouse's or partner's occupational status? Is he/she:

Employed full time or part time (Ask question 77)
Unemployed, but looking for a job (Ask question 77)
Not employed and not looking for a job (Skip to question 78)
Retired, student, homemaker (Skip to question 78)

(If employed or looking for a job, ask:)

77. What is his/her occupation? What kind of work does he/she normally do?

78. Do you have any children under 18?

Yes (Ask questions 79 and 80)
No (Skip to question 81)

(If yes to question 78, ask:)

79. How many children do you have under 18?

80. How many of them, if any, are under 6?

81a. Was your approximate total family income last   Under $20,000
      year: Over $20,000
                                                              Refused/don't know

(If under $20,000, ask:)

81b. Was it under or over $10,000?   Under $10,000
                                                         $10,000–$19,999
                                                         Refused

(If over $20,000, ask:)

81c. Was it under or over $30,000? $20,000–$29,999
                                                          $30,000 or more
                                                         Refused

82. To help us classify the answers, we'd like to know your racial and ethnic background. Are you Caucasian (white), Black, Asian, Hispanic, or a member of some other group?

83. Finally, I would like to ask you how you felt during   Very comfortable
     this interview. Would you say you felt: Fairly comfortable
                                                          Fairly uncomfortable
                                                          Very uncomfortable

84. It is possible that we might want to get some additional information for this survey . . . if we do, may we call you back one more time at a later date, possibly in six months to a year?

Thank you. May I please reconfirm your telephone number and have your first name or initials in case my supervisor needs to verify this interview?

Respondent first name/initials: _____   Respondent's sex:
                                                                   Male

Telephone number: _____   Female

Interviewer name: _____   Interviewer's sex:
                                                                   Male

Date: _____   Female

Cluster no. _____   Age of interviewer:
                                                               Under 18

Line no. _____   18–24
                                                               25–34

Time ended: _____   35–49
                                                             50–64
                                                                   65 and older

(Interviewer: please evaluate respondent's reaction to interview:)

Level of cooperation	Reluctance in answering sexual questions
Respondent was:	Respondent was:
Very cooperative	Very reluctant
Somewhat cooperative	Somewhat reluctant
Not very cooperative	Not very reluctant
Not at all cooperative	Not at all reluctant

References

Abbey, A. "Sex Differences in Attributions for Friendly Behavior: Do Males Misperceive Females' Friendliness?" *Journal of Personal and Social Psychology*, 1982, *47* (5), 830–838.

Babbie, E. *Survey Research Methods*. Belmont, Calif.: Wadsworth, 1973.

Barrett, N. S. "Women in the Job Market: Occupations, Earnings, and Career Opportunities." In R. E. Smith (ed.), *The Subtle Revolution*. Washington, D.C.: Urban Institute, 1979.

Bass, B., Krusall, J., and Alexander, R. A. "Male Managers' Attitudes Toward Working Women." *American Behavioral Scientist*, 1971, *15* (2), 221–236.

Bem, S. L. "Gender Schema Theory: A Cognitive Account of Sex Typing." *Psychological Review*, 1981, *88* (4), 354–364.

Benson, D. J., and Thomson, G. E. "Sexual Harassment on a University Campus: The Confluence of Authority Relations, Sexual Interest, and Gender Stratification." *Social Problems*, 1982, *29*, 236–251.

Berscheid, E., and Walster, E. "Physical Attractiveness." In L. Berkowitz (ed.), *Advances in Experimental Social Psychology*. Vol. 7. New York: Academic Press, 1974.

Blau, F. D. *Equal Pay in the Office*. Lexington, Mass.: Lexington Books, 1977.

Briar, S. "Welfare from Below: Recipients' Views of the Public Welfare System." In J. Tenbrook (ed.), *The Law of the Poor*. San Francisco: Chandler, 1966.

Burt, M. R. "Cultural Myths and Supports for Rape." *Journal of Personality and Social Psychology*, 1980, *38* (2), 217–230.

Cash, T. F., Kehr, J. A., Polyson, J., and Freeman, V. "Role of Physical Attractiveness in Peer Attribution of Psychological Disturbance." *Journal of Consulting and Clinical Psychology*, 1977, *45* (6), 987–993.

Collins, E. G. C., and Blodgett, T. B. "Sexual Harassment: Some See It . . . Some Won't." *Harvard Business Review*, 1981, *59* (2), 76–95.

Crowley, J., Levitin, T. E., and Quinn, R. P. "Seven Deadly Half-Truths About Women." In C. Tavris (ed.), *The Female Experience*. Del Mar, Calif.: CRM, 1973.

Dion, K., Berscheid, E., and Walster, E. "What Is Beautiful Is Good." *Journal of Personality and Social Psychology*, 1972, *24* (3), 285–290.

Drexler, J. A. "Organizational Climate: Its Homogeneity Within Organizations." *Journal of Applied Psychology*, 1977, *61* (1), 38–42.

Dunwoody-Miller, V., and Gutek, B. A. "Sexual Harassment in the State Workforce: Results of a Survey." Report to the California Commission on the Status of Women–SHE Project, 1985.

Equal Employment Opportunity Commission. *Interpretive Guidelines on Sexual Harassment*. March 11, 1980.

Etzkowitz, H. "The Male Sister: Sexual Separation of Labor in Society." *Journal of Marriage and the Family*, 1971, *33*, 431–434.

Fairhurst, G. T., and Snavely, B. K. "A Test of the Social Isolation of Male Tokens." *Academy of Management Journal*, 1983a, *26* (2), 353–361.

Fairhurst, G. T., and Snavely, B. K. "Majority and Token Minority Group Relationships: Power Acquisition and Communication." *Academy of Management Review*, 1983b, *8* (2), 292–320.

Farley, L. *Sexual Shakedown: The Sexual Harassment of Women on the Job*. New York: McGraw-Hill, 1978.

Feldberg, R., and Glenn, E. "Male and Female: Job Versus Gender Models in the Sociology of Work." *Social Problems*, 1979, *26*, 524–535.

Flaim, P. O., and Fullerton, H. N. "Labor Force Projections to

1990: Three Possible Paths." *Monthly Labor Review,* 1978, *101* (12), 25–35.

Gross, A. E. "The Male Role and Heterosexual Behavior." *Journal of Social Issues,* 1978, *34* (1), 87–107.

Groves, R., and Kahn, R. *Surveys by Telephone: A National Comparison with Personal Interviews.* New York: Academic Press, 1979.

Gutek, B. A. "Satisfaction Guaranteed: What Does It Mean?" *Social Policy,* 1978, *9,* 56–60.

Gutek, B. A. "A Psychological Examination of Sexual Harassment." In B. A. Gutek (ed.), *Sex-Role Stereotyping and Affirmative Action Policy: Problems, Processes, and Solutions.* Los Angeles: Institute of Industrial Relations, University of California, 1982.

Gutek, B. A., and Morasch, B. "Sex Ratios, Sex Role Spillover, and Sexual Harassment of Women at Work." *Journal of Social Issues,* 1982, *38* (4), 55–74.

Gutek, B. A., Morasch, B., and Cohen, A. G. "Interpreting Social Sexual Behavior in a Work Setting." *Journal of Vocational Behavior,* 1983, *22* (1), 30–48.

Gutek, B. A., and Nakamura, C. Y. "Gender Roles and Sexuality in the World of Work." In E. Allgeier and N. McCormick (eds.), *Gender Roles and Sexual Behavior: Changing Boundaries.* Palo Alto, Calif.: Mayfield, 1982.

Gutek, B. A., and others. "Sexuality and the Workplace." *Basic and Applied Social Psychology,* 1980, *1* (3), 255–265.

Handschumacher, I., and Gutek, B. A. "Interviewer Effects in Surveys Dealing with Sensitive Topics." Paper presented at Western Psychological Association Convention, Honolulu, May 1980.

Henley, N. M. *Body Politics: Power, Sex and Nonverbal Communication.* Englewood Cliffs, N.J.: Prentice-Hall, 1977.

Henley, N. M., and Mayo, C. (eds.). *Gender and Nonverbal Behavior.* New York: Springer-Verlag, 1981.

Herzberg, F., Fisher, C. D., and Taylor, M. S. "Consequences of Individual Feedback on Behavior in Organizations." *Journal of Applied Psychology,* 1979, *4,* 349–371.

Herzberg, F., Mausner, B., and Snyderman, B. *The Motivation to Work.* (2nd ed.) New York: Wiley, 1959.

Jacobs, J. A. "The Sex-Segregation of Occupations and the Career

Patterns of Women." Unpublished doctoral dissertation, Department of Sociology, Harvard University, 1983.

Jacobs, J. A. "Trends in Sex-Segregation in American Higher Education, 1948–1980." In L. Larwood, A. Stromberg, and B. A. Gutek (eds.), *Women and Work.* Beverly Hills, Calif.: Sage, 1985.

Janoff-Bulman, R. "Characterological Versus Behavioral Self-Blame: Inquiries into Depression and Rape." *Journal of Personality and Social Psychology,* 1979, *37* (10), 1798–1809.

Jensen, I. "Attributions and Assignment of Responsibility in Sexual Harassment." Unpublished doctoral dissertation, Department of Psychology, University of California at Los Angeles, 1981.

Jensen, I., and Gutek, B. A. "Attributions and Assignment of Responsibility in Sexual Harassment." *Journal of Social Issues,* 1982, *38* (4), 121–136.

Kanter, R. M. *Men and Women of the Corporation.* New York: Basic Books, 1977a.

Kanter, R. M. "Some Effects of Proportions in Group Life: Skewed Sex Ratios and Response to Token Women." *American Journal of Sociology,* 1977b, *2* (5), 965–990.

Katz, D., and Kahn, R. L. *The Social Psychology of Organizations.* (2nd ed.) New York: Wiley, 1978.

Khandwalla, P. N. *The Design of Organizations.* New York: Harcourt Brace Jovanovich, 1977.

Kish, L. *Survey Samples.* New York: Wiley, 1965.

Korda, M. "Sex at the Office." In D. S. David and R. Brannon (eds.), *The Forty-Nine Percent Majority: The Male Sex Role.* Reading, Mass.: Addison-Wesley, 1976.

Laws, J. L. "The Psychology of Tokenism: An Analysis." *Sex Roles,* 1975, *1,* 51–67.

Laws, J. L. *The Second X: Sex Role and Social Role.* New York: Elsevier, 1979.

Lindsey, K. "Sexual Harassment on the Job and How to Stop It." *Ms.,* 1977, *6,* 47–54.

Lipman-Blumen, J. "Toward a Homosocial Theory of Sex Roles: An Explanation of the Sex Segregation of Social Interaction." In M. Blaxall and B. Reagan (eds.), *Women and the Workplace.* Chicago: University of Chicago Press, 1976.

Lipman-Blumen, J. *Gender Roles and Power.* Englewood Cliffs, N. J.: Prentice-Hall, 1984.

McGuire, W. J., McGuire, C. V., Child, P. and Fujioka, T. "Salience of Ethnicity in the Spontaneous Self-Concept as a Function of One's Ethnic Distinctiveness in a Social Environment." *Journal of Personality and Social Psychology,* 1978, *36* (5), 511–520.

Macke, A. S. "Using the National Longitudinal Survey to Examine Changes in Women's Role Behavior." *Journal of Social Issues,* 1982, *38* (1), 39–51.

MacKinnon, C. *Sexual Harassment of Working Women: A Case of Sex Discrimination.* New Haven, Conn.: Yale University Press, 1979.

Madden, J. F. "Persistence of Pay Differentials: The Economics of Sex Discrimination." In L. Larwood, A. Stromberg, and B. A. Gutek (eds.), *Women and Work.* Beverly Hills, Calif.: Sage, 1985.

Martin, J., and Pettigrew, T. F. "Shaping the Organizational Context for Minority Inclusion." In J. McPartland and J. Campbell (eds.), *Minorities in High Technology Organizations,* in press.

Merton, R. K. *Social Theory and Social Structure.* (Rev. ed.) New York: Free Press, 1957.

Molloy, J. T. *Dress for Success.* Chicago: Follett, 1975.

Molloy, J. T. *The Woman's Dress for Success Book.* Chicago: Follett, 1977.

Nieva, V. F., and Gutek, B. A. *Women and Work: A Psychological Perspective.* New York: Praeger, 1981.

Nilson, L. B. "The Occupational and Sex-Related Components of Social Standing." *Sociology and Social Research,* 1976, *60* (3), 328–336.

Northcraft, G., and Martin, J. "Double Jeopardy: Resistance to Affirmative Action from Potential Beneficiaries." In B. A. Gutek (ed.), *Sex Role Stereotyping and Affirmative Action Policy: Problems, Processes, and Solutions.* Los Angeles: Institute for Industrial Relations, University of California, 1982.

Oppenheimer, V. "The Sex-Labeling of Jobs." *Industrial Relations,* 1968, *43* (2), 218–232.

Pearman, M. I., and Lebrato, M. T. *Sexual Harassment in Employment: Investigator's Guidebook.* Sacramento: California State Personnel Board and California Commission on the Status of Women, 1984.

Pennar, K., and Mervosh, E. "Women at Work: They've Reshaped the Economy—and Now Their Wages Will Rise." *Business Week,* Jan. 28, 1985, pp. 80–85.

Pettigrew, T. F. *Racially Separate or Together?* New York: McGraw-Hill, 1971.

Petty, M. M., and Lee, G. K. "Moderating Effects of Sex of Supervisor and Subordinate on Relationships Between Supervisory Behavior and Subordinate Satisfaction." *Journal of Applied Psychology,* 1975, *60* (5), 624–628.

Petty, M. M., and Miles, R. H. "Leader Sex-Role Stereotyping in Social Service Organizations." In R. L. Taylor and others (eds.), *Proceedings of the Annual Meeting of the Academy of Management.* Kansas City, Mo.: Academy of Management, 1976.

Pfeffer, J. *Organizations and Organization Theory.* Marshfield, Mass.: Pitman, 1982.

Pogrebin, L. C. "Sex Harassment: The Working Woman." *Ladies Home Journal,* June 4, 1977, p. 24.

Quinn, R. "Coping with Cupid: The Formation, Impact, and Management of Romantic Relationships in Organizations." *Administrative Science Quarterly,* 1977, *22* (1), 30–45.

Quinn, R., Gutek, B. A., and Walsh, J. T. "Telephone Interviewing: A Reappraisal and a Field Experiment." *Basic and Applied Social Psychology,* 1980, *1* (2), 127–153.

Quinn, R., and Shepard, L. *The 1972–73 Quality of Employment Survey: Descriptive Statistics with Comparison Data from the 1969–70 Survey of Working Conditions.* Ann Arbor: Institute for Social Research, University of Michigan, 1974.

Rivers, C. "Sexual Harassment: The Executive's Alternative to Rape." *Mother Jones,* 1978, *3* (5), 21–22, 24, 28–29.

Rosenbaum, J. E. "Persistence and Change in Pay Inequalities Between Men and Women: Implications for Job Evaluations and Comparable Worth." In L. Larwood, A. Stromberg, and B. A. Gutek (eds.), *Women and Work.* Beverly Hills, Calif.: Sage, 1985.

Safran, C. "What Men Do to Women on the Job." *Redbook,* Nov. 1976, pp. 149, 217–223.

Schneider, B. "Consciousness About Sexual Harassment Among

Heterosexual and Lesbian Women Workers." *Journal of Social Issues,* 1982, *38* (4), 75–97.

Schreiber, C. T. *Changing Places: Men and Women in Transitional Occupations.* Cambridge, Mass.: MIT Press, 1979.

Shure, G. H., and Meeker, R. J. "A Minicomputer System for Multiperson Computer-Assisted Telephone Interviewing." *Behavior Research Methods and Instrumentation,* 1978, *10* (2), 196–202.

Siegel, C. "Sex Differences in Occupational Choices of Second Graders." *Journal of Vocational Behavior,* 1973, *3* (1), 15–19.

Smith, E. R., Ferree, M. M., and Miller, F. D. "A Short Scale of Attitudes Toward Feminism." *Representative Research in Social Psychology,* 1975, *6,* 51–56.

Somers, A. "Sexual Harassment in Academe: Legal Issues and Definitions." *Journal of Social Issues,* 1982, *38* (4), 23–32.

Spangler, E., Gordon, M. A., and Pipkin, R. M. "Token Women: An Empirical Test of Kanter's Hypothesis." *American Journal of Sociology,* 1978, *85,* 160–175.

Staines, G. L., Pleck, J. H., Shepard, L. J., and O'Connor, P. "Wives' Employment Status and Marital Adjustment: Yet Another Look." *Psychology of Women Quarterly,* 1978, *3* (1), 90–120.

Tangri, S., Burt, M. R., and Johnson, L. B. "Sexual Harassment at Work: Three Explanatory Models." *Journal of Social Issues,* 1982, *38* (4), 55–74.

Taylor, S. E., and Fiske, S. T. "Salience, Attention, and Attribution: Top of the Head Phenomena." In L. Berkowitz (ed.), *Advances in Experimental Social Psychology.* New York: Academic Press, 1978.

Taylor, S. E., Fiske, S. T., Etcoff, N. L., and Ruderman, A. J. "Categorical and Contextual Bases of Person Memory and Stereotyping." *Journal of Personality and Social Psychology,* 1978, *36* (7), 778–793.

Treiman, D. J., and Hartmann, H. I. (eds.). *Women, Work and Wages: Equal Pay for Jobs of Equal Value.* Washington, D.C.: National Academy Press, 1981.

U.S. Department of Labor. *Perspectives on Working Women: A Databook.* Washington, D.C.: Bureau of Labor Statistics, U.S. Department of Labor, October 1980.

U.S. Department of Labor. *Time of Change: 1983 Handbook on Women Workers.* Bulletin no. 298. Washington, D.C.: U.S. Department of Labor, 1983.

U.S. Merit Systems Protection Board. *Sexual Harassment in the Federal Workplace: Is It a Problem?* Washington, D.C.: U.S. Government Printing Office, 1981.

Wallace, P. A. *Equal Employment Opportunity and the AT&T Case.* Cambridge, Mass.: MIT Press, 1976.

Index

211